# 如何帮助学生高效提高读后续写能力

## 写给教师的五五拍戏教学法

王 焕 周丽娟◎编著

**编委会**

**主 任** 王 焕 周丽娟

**副主任** 王燕艳 方 欣 谢婷婷 张 沁 褚 洁

**内容制作者**（按姓氏拼音排序）：

陈 希 丹 阳 龚鸿秀 潘 颖 彭亚楠 张志辉

**联合实践教师**（按姓氏拼音排序）：

安 梅 何 灿 李俊翔 李晓飞 刘 巧 王树彬 肖 璟

大连理工大学出版社

**图书在版编目(CIP)数据**

如何帮助学生高效提高读后续写能力：写给教师的五五拍戏教学法 / 王焕，周丽娟编著. -- 大连：大连理工大学出版社，2024. 12.（2025.1 重印）-- ISBN 978-7-5685-5242-4

Ⅰ. G633.412

中国国家版本馆 CIP 数据核字第 2024M5G294 号

大连理工大学出版社出版

地址：大连市软件园路 80 号　邮政编码：116023

营销中心：0411-84708842　0411-84707410　邮购及零售：0411-84706041

E-mail: dutp@dutp.cn　URL: https://www.dutp.cn

大连图腾彩色印刷有限公司印刷　　大连理工大学出版社发行

幅面尺寸:185mm×260mm　印张:7.25　字数:181 千字

2024 年 12 月第 1 版　2025 年 1 月第 2 次印刷

责任编辑:张晓燕　责任校对:孙　扬

封面设计:顾　娜

ISBN 978-7-5685-5242-4　定　价:38.00 元

# 前言

PREFACE

《普通高中英语课程标准（2017 年版 2020 年修订）》指出，语言技能是语言运用能力的重要组成部分，涵盖听、说、读、看、写五大核心技能。听、读和看属于理解性技能，说和写属于表达性技能。理解性技能和表达性技能在语言学习中相辅相成，相互促进。然而，在实际教学中，学生在衔接这两类技能方面仍面临诸多挑战，特别是在应对新高考读后续写题型时，这些问题尤为明显。

读后续写作为新高考的核心题型，不仅全面考查学生的阅读理解能力，而且对其语言组织能力、情节构思能力和思维连贯性提出了较高要求。然而，在备考读后续写题型的过程中，学生往往面临一些挑战：阅读理解能力不足，难以提炼出文本的关键信息；情节构思不清晰，难以构建连贯的故事情节；语言表达薄弱，语句衔接不畅，内容单一且缺乏深度。

与此同时，教师在指导学生进行读后续写练习时也面临多种挑战：教学方法单一；教学内容缺乏系统性；缺失有效的反馈机制，难以及时发现和改进学生问题；学生水平差异较大，难以兼顾；教师的专业能力存在一定局限性。

为了解决教师及学生在读后续写题型方面的困境，笔者编写了本书。

**一、本书内容介绍**

笔者精心挑选了 10 篇高考真题和优秀模拟题，并针对这些题目设计了一系列经过精心打磨的教学案例，旨在帮助教师突破读后续写的教学瓶颈。

为更好地支持教师开展读后续写教学，本书引入了以下创新教学法：

**1. 六何分析法**

结合“5W1H”（Who, When, Where, What, Why, How）六何分析法，帮助学生快速抓住文本的核心要素，提炼关键信息。该方法能够帮助学生在阅读和续写过程中厘清人物关系、情节发展、人物的情感变化，使得续写内容更加紧密和连贯。

**2. 五五拍戏教学法**

该方法将每段内容分解为 5 个句子，帮助学生系统地规划情节发展、人物行动和情感变化。通过逐步拆解，学生能够更清晰地构建完整的故事框架，有效避免情节脱节或逻辑不清的问题。

**3. 点线面润色升级法**

该方法通过从具体细节（点）到情节链条（线），再到多维度描写（面）的逐步训练，提升学生语言表达的层次感。通过递进式的练习，学生能够更加生动、精准地描绘人物的动作、情感、心理和环境，增强写作的表现力和深度。

**4. 科学的评价与反馈机制**

本书设置了系统的学生自评、同伴互评和教师反馈机制，确保学生在写作过程中能够及时发现并改进自己的不足。此外，针对续写中的常见问题，本书提供了具体的修改建议，教师可以借鉴案例中的修改建议，进而将此方法灵活运用到自己的实际教学中，指导学生优化文章结构和语言表达，从而有效提高写作水平。

**二、本书优质案例设计思路**

每个教学案例均由文本分析、学情分析、教学目标、教学思路和教学过程五大部分组成，并配有真题文本和参考范文，供教师参考。以下是各部分的具体设计思路：

**【文本分析】**文本分析是每个读后续写教学案例的基础。该部分内容聚焦语篇大意、叙事视角、叙事风格和主题语境，帮助学生深入理解原文结构和写作特点，为续写打下坚实的基础。

**【学情分析】**根据学生的实际情况进行设计，目的是帮助教师了解学生当前的学习水平和所面临的具体问题，从而制定有针对性的教学策略。

**【教学目标】**本书通过案例教学，明确教师在课堂中需要帮助学生实现的四个关键能力发展目标：语言能力、文化意识、思维品质、学习能力。

**【教学思路】**从任务型学习、情境创设等多角度指导教师开展高效、有序的课堂教学，激发学生的学习兴趣，提升他们的参与度。

**【教学过程】**教学过程是每一个案例的核心部分，该板块详细描述了每一节课的具体教学环节，帮助教师在实际教学中掌握清晰的步骤和操作指南。

本书旨在为广大一线教师提供科学、实用的教学方法和案例，帮助他们提升读后续写的教学效果和专业水平。

本书所有案例均由高中一线优秀教师精心研发与设计，并经过多轮修改与完善，以确保内容的科学性和实用性，供广大教师参考。限于时间与水平，书中难免存在疏漏之处，恳请各位读者和专家批评指正，以帮助我们不断完善内容，提升质量。

编　者

2024 年 12 月

# 目录

CONTENTS

# 第一章

## 读后续写分析及教学实施策略

# 第一节

# 读后续写分析

## 一 读后续写命题分析

为贯彻落实《国务院关于深化考试招生制度改革的实施意见》的要求，深化考试内容改革，高考英语学科自 2016 年开始，在综合改革试点省份启用了读后续写题型。读后续写作为英语学科新高考改革的一个重要题型已经逐渐在全国范围推广使用。

《普通高等学校招生全国统一考试英语科考试说明》（以下简称《考试说明》）对读后续写的界定：提供一段 350 词以内的语言材料，要求考生根据该材料内容、所给段落开头语和所标示关键词进行续写（150 词左右），将其发展成一篇与给定材料有逻辑衔接，情节和结构完整的短文。考查的主要内容包括以下四点：（1）与所给短文及段落开头语的衔接程度；（2）内容的丰富性和对所给关键词的覆盖情况；（3）应用语法结构和词汇的丰富性、准确性；（4）上下文的连贯性[①]。

读后续写作为一种教学手段和测试题型广受一线学者们的关注。读后续写的基本设计是让学习者阅读一篇删除结尾的文章并将其补全。其促学机制是协同（Wang & Wang，2015[②]），指在"续"创造的交际需要驱动下，学习者与文本深层互动、相互协调，使得语言高度配合，两者之间一高一低不对称的语言水平差距逐渐弥合，产生语言学习的"拉平效应"（王初明，2016[③]）。协同发生于情境模式和语言结构两个层面。为促进语言理解，

① 教育部考试中心 . 普通高等学校招生全国统一考试英语科考试说明（高考综合改革试验省份试用）[M]. 北京：高等教育出版社，2015.

② Wang, C. & Wang, M. Effect of alignment on L2 written production [J]. Applied Linguistics, 2015(5)：503-526.

③ 王初明，以"续"促学 [J]. 现代外语，2016(6)：784-793.

学习者对文本所处的情境，包括时空、意图、因果、人物等维度，会形成趋同的情境模式（Zwaan & Radvansky，1998[④]）。情境模式的协同通过结构启动机制，促进语言结构的协同，而语言结构的协同亦有助于情境模式的构建。结构启动指重复或模仿原文词语、句法结构的现象，这有助于强化和扩张学习者的语言表征，帮助学习者理解，进而学会新的语言结构（王初明，2014[⑤]）。

王初明较早提出外语写长法，主张用读后续写去激励学生写长文(王初明等，2000[⑥])，并提出“学伴用随”外语学习原则，为读后续写进一步提供了理论支撑(王初明，2009[⑦])。随后，不少学者开展相关实证研究表明，读后续写具有较为明显的促学作用(王初明，2015[⑧];姜琳、陈锦，2015[⑨]；王启，2021[⑩])。

读后续写是一种考查考生阅读与写作综合能力的试题，与应用文写作相比给考生更多发挥想象力、展示写作水平的空间。读后续写题型将阅读与写作结合，旨在考查考生对阅读文本的理解与分析，以及在此基础上合理创造内容并使用恰当、准确的语言进行书面表达的能力。读后续写需要考生具有一定的思维能力，在阅读时厘清故事情节发展的前因后果，分析人物表现出的内心情绪变化，解读作者的意图和目的，评价故事的文化价值[⑪]。

在读后续写中，阅读材料内容是语言输入，续写段落内容是语言输出。阅读是关键，续写是核心。学生只有精准、到位地解读原文文本，把握文本关键信息和语言特点，才能有逻辑地、合理地进行续写[⑫]。

王初明指出读后续写具有三项促学优势：（1）激发表达动机。续写任务中提供的文章内容不完整，能够激发学生的表达意愿，使其在创造内容的过程中将语言使用与篇章语境关联起来，加速提高语言表达能力。（2）凸显语境作用。续写紧随原文，伴随语篇情境，模仿前文写下文，利用前文提供的语境，确保内容的逻辑发展，并规范、得体地使用语言。

---

④ Zwaan, R. A. & Radvansky, G. A. Situation models in language comprehension and memory [J]. Psychological Bulletin, 1998(2)：162-185.

⑤ 王初明．内容要创造 语言要模仿——有效外语教学和学习的基本思路 [J]. 外语界，2014(2)：42-48.

⑥ 王初明，牛瑞英，郑小湘．以写促学——一项英语写作教学改革的试验 [J]. 外语教学与研究，2000(3)：207.

⑦ 王初明．学相伴用相随——外语学习的学伴用随原则 [J]. 中国外语，2009 (5)：53-59.

⑧ 王初明．读后续写何以有效促学 [J]. 外语教学与研究，2015(5)：753-762.

⑨ 姜琳，陈锦．读后续写对英语写作语言准确性、复杂性和流利性发展的影响 [J]. 现代外语，2015(3)：366-375.

⑩ 王启．读后续写协同产出的促学效果 [J]. 外语界，2021(6)：15-22.

⑪ 夏谷鸣．读后续写：英语学科核心素养的一种评价途径 [J]. 中小学外语教学（中学篇），2018（01）：01-06.

⑫ 宋颖超．读后续写教学中培养学生思维品质的策略 [J]. 中小学外语教学（中学篇），2017（12）：22-26.

（3）借力互动促学。考生在阅读时与文章及其作者互动，续写时内容产出与阅读理解互动，促使所写与所读协同，产生拉平效应。互动强度越大，拉平效应就越强，学习效果也就越好[13]。

## 二 读后续写题型分析

新课标全国 I 卷读后续写真题题干要求如下：

第二节：（满分 25 分）
阅读下列材料，根据其内容和所给段落开头语续写两段，使之构成一篇完整的短文。
注意：
1. 续写词数应为 150 个左右；
2. 请按如下格式在答题卡的相应位置作答。

## 三 读后续写真题分析

表 1–1–1 是近九年（2016—2024 年）高考英语读后续写题型的考查情况。

表 1–1–1　　2016—2024 年高考英语读后续写汇总

| 年份 | 卷别 | 体裁 | 主题 | 原文词数(个) | 续写故事前情概要 |
| --- | --- | --- | --- | --- | --- |
| 2024 年 | 新高考全国Ⅰ、Ⅱ卷 | 记叙文 | 人与社会 | 356 | “我”因飞机延误，深夜抵达维也纳。为了赶时间，“我”匆忙搭乘了 Gunter 的出租车，并在其帮助下成功到达车站，但“我”却无法支付其车费 |
|  | 浙江卷 1 月 | 记叙文 | 人与自我 | 324 | Eva 通过跑步领悟并用心理调节技巧辨识校园，适应校园 |
| 2023 年 | 新高考全国Ⅰ、Ⅱ卷 | 记叙文 | 人与自我 | 324 | “我”作为一名以英语为第二语言的中学生，在老师的鼓励下参加写作比赛，并通过努力取得优异的成绩 |
|  | 浙江卷 1 月 | 记叙文 | 人与自然 | 347 | “我”受邀去了农场，意外救下一只被困的蜂鸟。蜂鸟得救后，不愿离去，在“我”离开时，蜂鸟感恩并前来送行 |

⑬ 王初明. 读后续写何以有效促学 [J]. 外语教学与研究，2015（5）：753-762.

续表

| 年份 | 卷别 | 体裁 | 主题 | 原文词数(个) | 续写故事前情概要 |
|---|---|---|---|---|---|
| 2022年 | 新高考全国Ⅰ、Ⅱ卷 | 记叙文 | 人与自我 | 347 | “我”作为老师，帮助有残疾的 David 鼓起勇气，参加跑步比赛 |
| | 浙江卷6月 | 记叙文 | 人与社会 | 325 | “我”为了完成高中毕业所需的社区服务时间而参加社区志愿者活动 |
| | 浙江卷1月 | 记叙文 | 人与社会 | 345 | “我”被老师安排和一名性格孤僻但成绩优异的同学组队一起做项目 |
| 2021年 | 新高考全国Ⅰ卷 | 记叙文 | 人与自我 | 306 | 母亲节到了，一对双胞胎兄弟想亲自为母亲做早餐，给母亲一个惊喜，但由于是第一次做早餐，没有成功，Jeff 还烫伤了手 |
| | 浙江卷6月 | 记叙文 | 人与自我 | 315 | “我”在暑期打工，但不想像父亲期待的那样，上交打工报酬以补贴家用 |
| | 浙江卷1月 | 记叙文 | 人与自我 | 348 | 在万圣节，“我”与兄弟姐妹比赛看谁能带最大的南瓜回家。为了证明自己带的南瓜是最大的，“我”竟把自己的头塞进南瓜里，却怎么也拔不出来 |
| 2020年 | 新高考全国Ⅰ卷 | 记叙文 | 人与社会 | 325 | 为帮助 Bernard 走出困境，Mrs. Meredith 与孩子们一起制作爆米花让 Bernard 售卖 |
| | 浙江卷7月 | 记叙文 | 人与自然 | 330 | “我”和妻子 Elli 去拍摄北极熊，在营地遭遇了一头北极熊的袭击 |
| | 浙江卷1月 | 记叙文 | 人与自然 | 350 | 男孩去上大学了，狗狗 Poppy 回家后非常难过。男孩的父母为了安抚 Poppy，买了一只小狗给它做伴 |
| 2018年 | 浙江卷6月 | 记叙文 | 人与自然 | 325 | 父亲带我到叔叔的农场度假，我和父亲骑马外出迷了路 |
| 2017年 | 浙江卷11月 | 记叙文 | 人与自然 | 343 | 童年时，“我”与母亲的一次旅行经历 |
| | 浙江卷6月 | 记叙文 | 人与自然 | 348 | Eric 与朋友一起骑自行车出游，途中遭到狼的追击 |
| 2016年 | 浙江卷10月 | 记叙文 | 人与自然 | 335 | 夫妻俩野外游玩，因争吵而走散，女主人迷路，在野外独自度过夜晚 |

## 四 读后续写评分标准

《考试说明》中对读后续写部分的评分原则如下：

1. 本题总分为 25 分，按五个档次进行评分。

2. 评分时，应先根据作答的整体情况确定其所属的档次，然后以该档次的要求来综合衡量，确定或调整档次，最后给分。

3. 评分时，应从内容、词汇语法和语篇结构三个方面考虑，具体为：

① 续写内容的质量、完整性及与原文情境的融洽度；

② 所使用词汇和语法结构的准确性、恰当性和多样性；

③ 上下文的衔接和全文的连贯性。

4. 评分时，还应注意：

① 词数少于 120 的，酌情扣分；

② 书写较差以致影响阅读的，酌情扣分；

③ 单词拼写和标点符号是写作规范的重要方面，评分时应视其对交际的影响程度予以考虑，英、美拼写及词汇用法均可接受。

陈康与六位具有二语习得和语言测试研究背景并参与了高考英语读写结合题型研发设计工作的专家进行了一对一访谈，然后根据访谈结果整理出对读后续写题型考查目标的详细描述，见表 1-1-2（陈康，2019[14]）。

表 1-1-2　高考英语读后续写考查目标描述

| 考查能力 | 具体描述 |
|---|---|
| 阅读能力 | ◆ 能理解原文内容<br>◆ 能准确理解原文的篇章结构和关键信息<br>◆ 能深入理解原文的内容要素、内容发展、逻辑关系、语言特点等 |
| 写作能力 | 1. 内容产出<br>◆ 能在原文基础上创造新的内容<br>◆ 能与原文内容保持融洽，形成有效协同<br>2. 语言运用<br>◆ 能使用丰富的词汇和句子结构并且使用得准确、恰当<br>◆ 与原文的词汇和句子结构甚至语言风格协同（较高要求）<br>3. 篇章结构<br>◆ 能与原文合理衔接<br>◆ 能使用恰当的连接手段使续写完整、连贯 |
| 思维能力 | ◆ 能在根据原文进行续写时体现出创造性 |
| 学习能力 | ◆ 能通过读后续写学习原文作者的语言特点和写作方式 |

⑭ 陈康. 高考英语概要写作与读后续写考查目标对比研究［J］. 中小学英语教学与研究，2019(4): 65-68.

读后续写题型在高考英语试卷中的分值为25分，按五个档次进行评分，见表1-1-3。

表1-1-3 读后续写分档标准

| 档次 | 要求 |
| --- | --- |
| 第五档<br>（21~25分） | 1. 与所给短文融洽度高，与所提供各段落开头语衔接非常合理，文章内容新颖、丰富、合理，非常有逻辑性，续写内容完整<br>2. 语法结构和词汇丰富、准确，语言错误很少，且完全不影响意义表达<br>3. 自然有效地使用了语句间的连接成分，使所续写文章结构紧凑，全文结构非常清晰，前后呼应，意义非常连贯 |
| 第四档<br>（16~20分） | 1. 与所给短文融洽度较高，与所提供各段落开头语衔接较为合理，比较有逻辑性，续写内容比较完整<br>2. 语法结构和词汇较为丰富、准确，表达比较流畅，可能有些许错误，但不影响意义表达<br>3. 比较有效地使用了语句间的连接成分，使所续写文章结构紧凑，全文结构比较清晰，意义比较连贯 |
| 第三档<br>（11~15分） | 1. 与所给短文关系较为密切，与所提供各段落开头语有一定程度的衔接，与原文情境基本相关，但有的情节不够合理或逻辑性不强<br>2. 语法结构和词汇能满足任务的要求，有一些错误，个别部分影响意义表达<br>3. 应用简单的语句间连接成分，使上下文内容连贯，全文结构基本清晰 |
| 第二档<br>（6~10分） | 1. 与所给短文有一定的关系，与所提供各段落开头语有一定程度的衔接，内容和逻辑上有一些问题，续写内容不够完整<br>2. 语法结构单调，词汇单一，有些语法结构和词汇方面的错误影响了意义的表达<br>3. 较少使用语句间的连接成分，全文内容缺少连贯性，全文结构不清晰，意义欠连贯 |
| 第一档<br>（1~5分） | 1. 与所提供短文和开头语的衔接较差，内容和逻辑上有较多重大问题，或有部分内容抄写原文，续写不完整，与原文情境脱节<br>2. 语法结构单调，词汇很有限，有较多语法结构和词汇方面的错误，严重影响了意义的表达<br>3. 缺乏语句间的连接成分，全文结构不清晰，意义不连贯 |
| 0分 | 未作答；所写内容太少或无法看清以致无法评判；所写内容全部抄自原文或与题目要求完全不相关 |

# 第二节 读后续写教学实施策略

## 一 读后续写教学现状

在日常教学实践中，笔者对学生的读后续写习作和教师的指导方法进行了深入观察，发现了一系列挑战和问题。这些问题不仅体现在学生在续写过程中遇到的困难上，也反映了教师在指导这一任务时面临的问题。

### （一）学生续写习作中的主要问题

#### 1. 与所给短文的融洽度

学生在读后续写习作中面临的融洽度挑战涉及多个层面，包括内容的逻辑一致性、风格的恰当模仿、主题的准确传达，以及续写段落开头语的有效衔接。

（1）续写内容与原文不连贯：学生往往因为浏览原文速度过快而未能充分捕捉原文的关键信息，导致续写内容与原文在故事线和细节上不连贯。同时，学生往往未能有效地利用或衔接续写段落的开头语等原文提供的线索，导致续写内容脱节。

（2）续写风格与原文不一致：学生续写时容易出现时态混乱、过度使用对话或生搬硬套一些背诵的高级语言和句式，导致续写内容的风格和原文不一致。

（3）续写主题与原文不一致：学生未能深入理解原文的深层含义，在续写时难以准确传达原文的主题思想。续写的主题容易偏离原文，难以体现出深刻的思想、积极的价值观和正能量，从而影响作品的整体质量和深度。

#### 2. 内容的丰富性和逻辑性

学生面临的关键挑战之一是其创作的内容既要丰富又要有逻辑性。常见问题包括：

（1）续写内容单薄且笼统：学生的续写内容往往缺乏深度，未能有效扩展或深化原文的主题。有时，续写内容甚至脱离原文的故事主线，显得过于泛泛且不符合生活逻辑。

（2）续写内容缺乏逻辑性：学生的续写内容经常出现不合理的情节设置，例如故事发展突兀或复杂混乱，缺乏清晰的逻辑联系。人物行为和情节进展通常也缺乏合理的解释或动机，导致整个故事线索难以令人信服。

**3. 语言的准确性和丰富性**

在语言的准确性和丰富性方面，学生的续写习作主要存在以下问题：

（1）续写词汇使用局限：学生在续写时往往忽视原文的语言特征和表达方式，常将背诵的好词好句生搬硬套，而不是使用与原文主题相符的词汇和表达方式。此外，频繁的语言错误也严重影响了意义的清晰表达。

（2）续写语法结构单一：学生的续写内容使用的语法结构通常过于单一，这导致语言表达显得单调，缺乏变化和深度。

**4. 上下文的连贯性**

在上下文连贯性方面，学生的续写习作主要存在以下问题：

（1）续写内容衔接不连贯：学生的续写内容常缺乏恰当的连接词和过渡句，导致续写内容衔接断裂，影响文本的整体性和意义表达。

（2）续写内容的结构松散：学生经常使用不恰当的主题句式不使用过渡句，使得其内容整体结构松散且不清晰，进而影响续写内容的逻辑性和易读性。

### （二）教师指导读后续写存在的问题

**1. 评价标准的不明确和反馈的不具体：**由于读后续写题型的开放性和主观性，教师在评价学生习作时常缺乏明确和统一的评价标准。教师的评价语言往往笼统并依赖个人经验，使学生难以了解具体需要改进的方面，从而影响他们对自己写作能力的准确评估和进一步提升。

**2. 教学方法单一，过分强调技巧背诵：**一些教师可能倾向于让学生机械地学习和背诵描写技巧等应试技巧，忽视培养他们的创造力和批判性思维能力。这导致读后续写走向死记硬背的道路，不利于学生语言能力的全面发展。

综上所述，学生的主要问题包括：续写内容与原文不连贯、风格和主题不一致、内容单薄和缺乏逻辑性、语言的准确性和丰富性不足，以及上下文连贯性欠佳等。教师的主要问题体现在评价标准的不明确和反馈的不具体性，以及教学方法的单一性和过分强调技巧背诵。这些问题不仅影响了学生续写作品的质量，也影响了他们写作能力的发展和创新思维的培养。

## 二 续写策略

基于读后续写教学的现状，本书从培养学生写作能力和提升教师指导水平两方面提供相应的策略，旨在提升读后续写的教学效果和学生的写作水平。

针对学生习作存在的问题，本书主要借助以下策略引导学生提高续写习作的质量。

### （一）六何分析法

本书采用六何分析法系统地开展语篇分析，培养学生的文本分析能力，提高他们的语言敏感性，以及加强对文本主题深层次解读和情感共鸣的引导。

六何分析法，又称六何学分析法或 5W1H 分析法，始于美国。1948 年，政治学家拉斯韦尔提出“5W 分析法”[①]。经过后续学者和实践者的不断研究、提炼、总结，此方法逐步发展为成熟的“5W+1H”模式。此分析法是一种综合性分析与问题解决的工具，其应用范围广泛，涵盖管理学、市场营销、项目规划、新闻采编等多个领域。该方法深入探讨“何事”（What）、“为何”（Why）、“何人”（Who）、“何时”（When）、“何地”（Where）、“如何”（How）六大基本问题，旨在全面且系统地理解与分析问题，进而促成更为有效的决策过程。六何分析法的优势在于其全面性与系统性，使使用该方法者能够从多维度分析问题，确保其决策和执行过程中可充分考虑关键要素。

在英语记叙文教学中，六何分析法有助于学生更好地理解和分析文本。分析维度包括：

1. 场景设定（Where）：分析故事发生的地点和场景，包括自然环境和社会环境，探讨其对故事情节及人物行为的影响。故事在哪里发生？这个地点对故事有什么影响？它如何影响故事中的人物和事件的发展？

2. 时间线（When）：关注故事的时间线及其对事件发展的影响。故事是何时发生的？时间的变化对故事有什么影响？

3. 人物剖析（Who）：分析故事的主要和次要人物，探究其性格特点、动机、行为和反应。这些角色的性格特点是什么？他们的行为和决定对故事有什么影响？

4. 情节梳理（What）：借助故事山梳理故事基本情节。文章主要讲了什么？故事的主要事件是什么？情节的起承转合是怎样的？故事的情节线和情感线是如何变化的？

5. 叙述视角与风格（How）：关注故事的叙述视角和风格。叙述视角可以是第一人称，使读者直接接触叙述者的个人感受；第二人称，创造一种对话感；第三人称，提供更

① 拉斯韦尔. 传播在社会中的结构与功能 [M]. 北京：中国传媒大学出版社，2012.

广阔的视野或仅限于特定人物的视角。叙述风格涉及故事的语言构成，包括词汇选择、句子结构和描述细节的程度，这三点共同确定了文本的情感调性和理解难度。风格可以是正式的——使用精练语言和复杂结构；或非正式的——更加口语化且直接。故事是从哪个角度叙述的？这种叙述角度对故事有什么影响？故事的叙述风格是怎样的？它如何影响故事的氛围和读者对故事的理解？

6. 情感态度与价值观（Why）：分析文本所蕴含的情感态度和价值观念，探索和理解作者的写作目的及文本传达的深层信息。文本中作者想要传递的深层信息和写作目的是什么？故事传递的价值观是什么？

通过六何分析法，学生能够全方位地深入分析英语记叙文，从而更好地理解文本的深层含义和作者的意图。学生分析所给文本与展开续写时，务必注意续写段落的提示句，这些提示句往往涉及新的人物或场景，是理解和续写文本的关键。具体操作方法详见表 1-2-1。

表 1-2-1　以六何分析法分析 2022 年新高考Ⅰ、Ⅱ卷读后续写真题

| 维度 | 具体内容 | 示例 |
| --- | --- | --- |
| Where | 故事发生在一个小镇附近的茂密常绿森林中，这里正在举行一场大型的越野长跑比赛。此场景象征着成长和挑战，森林作为自然环境，象征着难以预测的挑战和成长的旅程 | the route through a thick evergreen forest near a small town |
| When | 故事发生在越野长跑的当天，这个特定时间突出了赛事的重要性和紧迫感，以及对参与者的影响 | the day of the big cross-country run through the thick evergreen forest |
| Who | David：一个有大脑病患的十岁男孩，“独自站在一边，靠着篱笆”，平时的“大大的露出牙齿的笑容今天不见了”。David 的身体状况影响了他的运动能力。尽管如此，他“总是尽其所能参加他们做的任何事情”，这显示了他不受身体局限、不屈不挠的精神和积极参与的态度。特教老师：作为故事的叙述者和 David 的特教老师，他 / 她对 David 面临的挑战很清楚，并且对他的坚定决心感到自豪。特教老师对 David 给予了关心、支持和理解 | David：optimistic, determined, courageous, resilient and inspirational<br>I (the special teacher): empathetic, caring and protective |
| What | 故事主要讲述了 David 面对体育挑战的故事。尽管身体有障碍，他依然坚持加入越野长跑队并完成每次训练。情节展现了：起——David 决定不参赛，承——教练和特教老师的介入，转——David 最终决定参赛，合——强调他的坚持和努力 | Story mountain model（详见图 1-2-1） |

续表

| 维度 | 具体内容 | 示例 |
|---|---|---|
| How | 叙述视角：特教老师的第一人称视角<br>叙述风格：<br>1. 具体：文中对环境和人物状态的描述较为详细，如对跑步现场、David 的身体状况和情感状态的描述<br>2. 直接：叙述者直接表达了对 David 的同情和对某些事情的反应，如对教练决策的挫败感和对 David 坚持的自豪<br>3. 简洁：文本使用了容易理解的语言，没有过多使用复杂的修辞手法 | Narrative perspective: I<br>Narrative style:<br>1. Specific: David had a brain disease which prevented him from walking or running like other children, but at school, his classmates treated him like any other kid.<br>2. Direct: I bit back my frustration. I knew the coach meant well — he thought he was doing the right thing.<br>3. Brief: He was small for ten years old. His usual big toothy smile was absent today. |
| Why | 作者通过 David 的故事传递坚持与勇气、自主与自决、包容与平等等价值观。这些价值观不仅体现了作者对于个体挑战的深刻理解，也映射了一种理想的社会态度，即无论个体的限制如何，都应当鼓励他们充分参与并尊重他们的选择。通过这种方式，故事不仅提供了情感共鸣，也促进了对于更广泛社会问题的思考 | **Perseverance and Courage:** Despite the physical limitations caused by a brain disease, David chose to participate in the cross-country running event.<br>**Autonomy and Self-Determination:** The plot involving David's initial decision not to run, followed by his change of mind, highlighted the importance of personal autonomy and self-determination.<br>**Inclusiveness and Equality:** Although David's physical abilities differed from those of other children, he was seen as a regular kid at school, and his participation was not viewed as unusual by his classmates. This highlighted a societal acceptance of differences and the value that everyone should have equal opportunities to participate. |

## （二）故事山

梳理故事情节时，笔者借助“故事山”模型引导学生系统地分析故事的情节线及情感线，并预测续写内容的发展走向。具体步骤如下：

1. 开端（Beginning）：开端阐述背景信息和基本前提条件，为故事情节的展开奠定必要的场景和基础。同时，开端还呈现主要人物的初步情感状态，奠定故事的情感背景。

2. 发展（Development）：在故事发展阶段，一系列事件推动情节向前发展，同时情感线随着人物的互动发生变化。

3. 冲突（Conflict）：故事中的关键事件和主要问题所在。冲突是推动故事发展的动力。

冲突既可以是人物内心的矛盾，也可以是人物与外界势力的对抗，是构成故事高潮的关键因素。冲突阶段是情节和情感的集中爆发点，冲突的描述通常紧密结合人物的情感反应，展现人物的内心斗争和情感变化。

4. 解决（Resolution）：此阶段标志着故事冲突的逐步解决，推动故事向终点推进。解决阶段涵盖了冲突的解决、人物的转变及故事向结局的过渡。随着冲突的化解，情节线和情感线共同描绘了人物内心的成长和情感变化。

5. 结局（Ending）：结局既要呈现问题的最终解决和故事的圆满结尾，也要展现主要人物情感旅程的高潮，反映其经历变化后的情感状态与人生观。

通过深入理解"故事山"模型的各个环节，学生能够更准确地把握故事的情节与情感发展脉络。情节线与情感线的精细融合使得学生在分析故事情节的同时，能够深入挖掘角色的内心世界，确保续写作品在吸引读者的同时，也能与读者在情感层面产生共鸣。具体案例详见表 1-2-2。

表 1-2-2　　2022 年新高考Ⅰ、Ⅱ卷真题的故事山

| 环节 | 情节 | 情感 |
| --- | --- | --- |
| 开端（Beginning） | 一场大型的越野长跑赛正在准备中，学生们热身，David 独自站在一边 | David 没有他常有的笑容，显得孤独和不安 |
| 发展（Development） | 特教老师注意到 David 的犹豫，询问原因；学校教练透露了他对 David 可能面临挑战的担忧 | David 的犹豫表明他的内心冲突，害怕或不自信 |
| 冲突（Conflict） | David 面临的内心矛盾成了故事的主要冲突——他努力训练却决定退出比赛 | David 决定不参赛表明他对失败或被嘲笑的恐惧 |
| 解决（Resolution） | 故事并未完全展示解决的过程，但续写所提供的两句话提示了 David 可能会重新考虑参赛的决定 | David 在教练和老师的支持下可能重建信心 |
| 结局（Ending） | 文本中没有具体的结局，留给读者想象空间或续写的可能性 | 故事的情感走向暗示了一种正向的转变，可能是向着坚持和勇气的方向发展 |

通过梳理故事的情节线和情感线，学生不仅能够追踪故事情节的高潮和转折，还能够理解文中人物的内心世界。在续写时，学生可以考虑如何解决或进一步发展文中的冲突，并描绘出 David 的情感历程（图 1-2-1）。

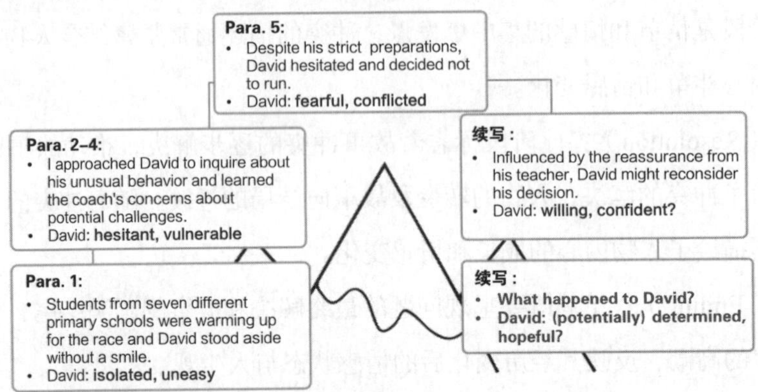


图 1-2-1 2022 年新高考Ⅰ、Ⅱ卷真题的故事山

## （三）五五拍戏教学法

为帮助学生构建合理且引人入胜的故事情节和结局，笔者运用“五五拍戏教学法”作为构建续写框架的核心方法。该方法旨在通过精确确定角色及其出场顺序，合理安排故事结构，协助学生构建一个明确的、可操作的续写结构框架。

“五五拍戏教学法”将读后续写的过程比喻为拍摄电影，学生担任导演的角色，决定哪些角色参与演出、确定出场顺序、如何表演等关键因素。该名称中的“五五”代表两个核心思路。第一个“五”指给学生明确指令，即每个续写段落只需要包含五句话（注：结合具体语篇可增减一句）；另一个“五”明确拍摄过程的逻辑顺序，即依托承上启下的原则，预测故事结局，提升情感态度和价值观的表达。通过将这五个场景的顺序设定为固定，另外五句话则结合前后句进行内容预设（注：戏份不够，细节或环境来凑），在一定程度上减轻学生的续写压力。具体案例详见图 1-2-2。

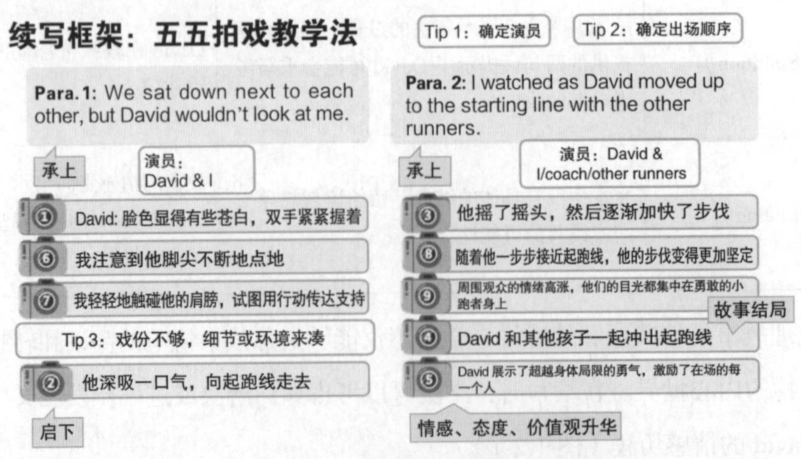


图 1-2-2 2022 年新高考Ⅰ、Ⅱ卷真题续写框架

根据提供的段首句，明确续写段落的主要演员：第一段以 David 和“我”为核心，第二段则加入其他参赛者，与 David 和“我”共同推动情节发展。同时，根据段首句确定演员的出场顺序，并合理设置拍摄场景。

场景 1：依托承上原则，承接第一段的段首句，聚焦 David 的心理状态和肢体动作（如 David 脸色有些苍白，双手紧紧握着）。

场景 2：依托启下原则，与第二段段首句衔接，即描述 David 克服内心障碍并采取行动（如深吸一口气，起身走向起跑线）。

场景 3：依托承上原则，承接第二段的段首句，即描述 David 接下来的具体行动（如他摇了摇头，然后逐渐加快了步伐）。

场景 4：呈现故事的结局（如 David 在突破心理障碍后与其他选手一起起跑）。

场景 5：故事的最后一幕，结合内心独白或旁白，升华整个故事的主题（如 David 战胜恐惧，展现成长与突破，传递信心和勇气，完成情感的升华和价值观的体现）。

场景 1 至场景 5 是续写的核心框架，呈现从情节起点（David 的紧张情绪）到情感高潮（比赛起跑）再到主题升华（成长与勇气）的完整过程。其他情节可围绕这五个核心场景展开，结合环境、动作和心理描写，为框架注入更多细节，丰富叙事层次。承上启下原则贯穿始终，每个场景紧密连接段首句和前后情节，确保续写内容逻辑清晰、流畅连贯。

### （四）点线面润色升级法

为了帮助学生有效地扩充其续写内容，笔者采用点线面润色升级法帮助学生丰富续写的文本内容并提高语言表达的准确性和多样性。具体原则详见表 1-2-3，具体案例详见表 1-2-4。

表 1-2-3　　点线面润色升级法

| 维度 | 原则 | 示例 |
| --- | --- | --- |
| 点 | 具体的某个动作 | She proudly raised her trophy high above her head. |
| 线 | 拆解单一动作，形成一连串的动作链 | She approached the stage, bowed to the audience and proudly raised her trophy high above her head. |
| 面 | 从外貌、环境、语言、心理活动等多个角度进行细致描写，使人物的形象、性格和动作更加立体 | ① The girl held her breath for a moment before lifting her trophy high above her head, a wave of gratitude and excitement rushing through her as she thought about the recognition of her hard work and dedication.【心理描写】<br>② She approached the stage and acknowledged the audience with a bow, saying, “Thank you, Mr. Black. Without your encouragement, I would never have found a writer inside me.”【语言描写】 |

表 1-2-4　　2022 年新高考Ⅰ、Ⅱ卷真题

| 列草稿 | 升级表达 | 升级思路 |
|---|---|---|
| His face was pale, and his hands were tightly clasped. | His face was pale, and his hands were tightly clasped, revealing his nervousness and unease. | 面：+ 心理描写（非谓语结构） |
| I noticed his toes tapping on the ground. | I noticed his toes tapping on the ground, a habit he has when he's anxious. | 面：+ 心理描写（状语从句） |
| I gently touched his shoulder, trying to offer some support. | I gently touched his shoulder, trying to offer some support, and whispered, "You don't have to do this if you're not ready." | 面：+ 语言描写（直接引语） |
| He took a deep breath and walked determinedly towards the starting line. | After a moment of silence, he took a deep breath, slowly stood up and walked determinedly towards the starting line, his eyes shimmering with newfound confidence. | 线：动作链（+ 状语）<br>面：+ 外貌描写（独立主格结构） |
| He shook his head, and then began to quicken his pace. | He shook his head as if to chase away the fears inside him, and then began to quicken his pace. | 面：+ 心理描写（虚拟语气） |
| As he approached the starting line, his steps became more determined. | As he approached the starting line, his steps became more determined, and his confidence seemed to grow. | 面：+ 心理描写（无灵主语） |
| The excitement of the crowd around us built up and their eyes all were on the brave young runner. | The excitement of the crowd around us built up, the atmosphere charged with expectation, and their eyes all were on the brave young runner. | 面：+ 环境描写（独立主格结构） |
| David and the other children rushed from the starting line. | As the starting gun sounded, David and the other children burst from the starting line, his decisive leap marking the beginning of his own hero's journey. | 点：精准化动作描写<br>面：+ 环境描写（状语从句）<br>+ 动作描写（独立主格结构） |
| David not only showed everyone his courage to overcome physical limitations but also inspired everyone present. | In that moment, not only did David show everyone his courage to overcome physical limitations, but he also inspired everyone present. | 点：精准化表达（倒装句） |
| 注意：并非所有的句子都需要升级。为了突出升级思路，笔者将此案例中的每个句子都做了升级 | | |

## （五）连句成篇

针对学生在续写习作中出现的上下文连贯性的问题，笔者借助连句成篇的方法引导学生有效地使用连接词、过渡句及其他用于语句间的连接成分，增强续写段落和全文的连贯性。具体案例详见图 1-2-3 和图 1-2-4。

**连句成篇技巧**

词：副词；并列连词

短语：介词短语；分词短语

句子：状语从句；定语从句；名词性从句

图 1-2-3 连句成篇技巧

**连句成篇**

| 连接成分 | | |
|---|---|---|
| 词 | 短语 | 句子 |
| ③ | ①②④⑥⑧ | ⑤⑦ |

***Paragraph 1*: *We sat down next to each other, but David wouldn't look at me*.** His face was pale, and his hands were tightly clasped. ① **Apart from these**, I noticed his toes tapping on the ground, a habit he has when he's anxious, which made me more concerned about him. ② **Sensing his discomfort**, I gently touched his shoulder and whispered, "You don't have to do this if you're not ready." ③ **Soon**, the preparatory whistle blew. ④ **Much to my surprise,** he took a deep breath, slowly stood up, and walked towards the starting line, his eyes filled with newfound confidence.

***Paragraph 2*: *I watched as David moved up to the starting line with the other runners*.** He shook his head as if to chase away the fears inside him and then began to quicken his pace. ⑤ **As he approached the starting line**, his steps became more determined, and ⑥ **after hearing the cheers from the crowd**, his confidence seemed to grow even stronger. ⑦ **The minute the starting gun sounded**, David and the other children burst from the starting line. ⑧ **At that very moment**, not only did David show everyone his courage to overcome physical limitations, but he also inspired everyone present.

图 1-2-4 2022 年新高考Ⅰ、Ⅱ卷真题连句成篇

## 三 讲评策略

针对上述提到的读后续写教师教学指导的问题，笔者采用以下策略提升评价效果并丰富教学方法，促进学生读后续写能力的全面提升，激发其创造性思维和提升其批判性分析能力，最终提高其写作水平。

### （一）设定明确的评价标准

根据第一章提供的评分档次及其对应的评价标准，读后续写主要考查四个方面：续写内容与所给短文的融洽度，内容的丰富性和逻辑性，语言的准确性和丰富性及上下文的连贯性。教师可将读后续写的评价标准细化为更详尽的评分细则，使评价过程更加透明且具有指导性，见表 1-2-5。

表 1-2-5　　　　细化的读后续写评分细则

| 评分档次 | 与所给短文的融洽度 | 内容的丰富性和逻辑性 | 语言的准确性和丰富性 | 上下文的连贯性 |
| --- | --- | --- | --- | --- |
| 第五档（21~25分） | 与所给短文融洽度高，与所提供各段落开头语衔接非常合理 | 内容新颖、丰富、合理，非常有逻辑性且完整 | 语法结构和词汇丰富、准确，语言错误较少，完全不影响意义的表达 | 有效地使用了语句间的连接成分，全文结构紧凑、清晰，意义连贯 |
| 第四档（16~20分） | 与所给短文融洽度较高，与所提供各段落开头语衔接较为合理 | 内容比较丰富，比较有逻辑性，比较完整 | 语法结构和词汇较为丰富、准确，可能有些许错误，但不影响意义的表达 | 比较有效地使用了语句间的连接成分，全文结构紧凑、比较清晰，意义比较连贯 |
| 第三档（11~15分） | 与所给短文关系较为密切，与所提供各段落开头语有一定程度的衔接 | 内容与原文情境基本相关，但有的情节不够合理或逻辑性不强 | 语法结构和词汇能够满足任务的要求，有一些错误，个别错误影响意义的表达 | 运用简单的语句间的连接成分，全文结构基本清晰，意义基本连贯 |
| 第二档（6~10分） | 与所给短文有一定关系，与所提供各段落开头语有一定衔接 | 逻辑有一些问题，内容不够完整 | 语法结构单调，运用的词汇有限，存在语法结构与词汇方向的错误，影响意义的表达 | 较少使用语句间的连接成分，全文结构不清晰，意义欠连贯 |
| 第一档（1~5分） | 与所给短文融洽度低，与所提供各段落开头语的衔接较差 | 逻辑上存在较多重大问题，或抄写了原文部分内容，内容不完整，与原文情境脱节 | 语法结构单调，词汇匮乏，有较多语法结构和词汇方面的错误，严重影响意义的表达 | 缺乏语句间的连接成分，全文结构不清晰，意义不连贯 |

教师可借助表1-2-5引导学生进行自评和互评，并润色、完善自己和同伴的习作。随后，教师要根据学生自评和互评的实际情况对学生习作进行恰当的点评。

## （二）提供具体、有益的反馈

在评价学生习作时，教师需要避免使用模糊和笼统的语言，应具体指出作品的优点和需要改进之处。例如，教师点评时不能简单地说“写得好”，应结合评分细则的四个维度指出学生习作需要改进之处，并引导学生借助前面的续写策略进行改进。

## （三）采用多样化的教学方法

教师应结合讲授、讨论、小组合作、案例分析等多种教学方法，激发学生的兴趣和参与度，提高他们的续写能力。

首先，教师需要重点教授学生如何根据不同写作任务和目的选择合适的写作策略，包括如何构思故事、如何发展角色和情节、如何使用语言表达复杂情感等，而非单一强调技巧的背诵。

其次，教师在日常教学中可以进行微场景写作练习，提供场景式写作任务，鼓励学生进行不同话题的写作，而非仅仅模仿和背诵范文。

最后，教师需要引导学生借助细化的读后续写评分细则（见表 1-2-5）进行同伴互评，提供和接受反馈，并引导学生进行自我反思，认识到自己的写作强项和待改进之处。具体案例如下。

### 微场景写作练习案例——成长类

请根据所给的情节，尝试续写故事的后续情节。（词数：150 个左右）

Amy, a middle school student, has recently faced bullying at school, affecting both her academic performance and social interactions. Feeling isolated and scared, Amy records her insecurity and loneliness in her diary, expressing concerns that the situation might worsen.

Para. 1 : Seated alone at the back of the library, Amy finally texted her favorite teacher. ____

________________________________________________________________

Para. 2 : Weeks later, Amy stood before her class to share her story. ________________

________________________________________________________________

参考范文：

**Seated alone at the back of the library, Amy finally texted her favorite teacher**. Within minutes, her teacher replied with more than just comforting words. She arranged for Amy to have weekly sessions with the school counselor, and organized an anti-bullying workshop for all students. Encouraged by her teacher, Amy felt that she wasn't fighting this battle alone anymore. Although she knew the road ahead would be challenging, her teacher gave her newfound strength to face the upcoming days.

**Weeks later, Amy stood before her class to share her story**. She began by recalling her initial feelings of helplessness, then described her meetings with the counselor and the difficult conversations that followed with her peers. With each detail, she emphasized the importance of seeking help and standing up against bullying. As she concluded her story, her classmates erupted into applause, deeply moved by her courage and resilience. Walking back to her seat, Amy felt a deep sense of relief and empowerment, her smile genuine and wide as she realized the impact of her voice.

# 第二章

## 读后续写教学设计优质案例

# 第一节

# 以2024年1月浙江卷为例的读后续写教学设计案例

## 一、文本分析

What 本文的主题语境是“人与自我”，主题群为“生活与学习”，话题内容涉及“克服困难，提升自我”。本文讲述了高中新生 Eva 在适应学校生活时所面临的两大挑战及其采取的相应的策略。首先，由于方向感差，她在错综复杂的校园建筑中迷路，因而选择只记住教室位置而忽略其他地方。其次，她在体育课上面对必须完成跑一英里的任务时感到不安和恐惧。然而，通过采用心理策略，她最终成功完成了挑战。

续写第一段的段首句：当 Pitt 教练在终点线对 Eva 说“干得好”时，她感到了吃惊。

续写第二段的段首句：Eva 决定使用同样的心理调节技巧来应对学校的复杂布局。

根据两段续写的首句内容，可以预测后面的故事情节：Eva 成功跑完了一英里。

What 教练的表扬让 Eva 意识到，专注于短期目标有助于她克服看似无法完成的任务。受到这一经验的启发，Eva 决定将这一策略应用到学校的导航问题上。她从记住每一层楼的布局开始，逐步扩大范围，最终成功克服了迷路的困扰。

Why 本文通过讲述 Eva 适应新环境并克服挑战的过程，鼓励读者在面对困难时，不应因任务庞大而退缩，而应将其拆解成小步骤，并逐步完成。

How 故事采用第三人称视角，讲述了 Eva 在面对困难时的心理变化与应对过程，从焦虑到逐步克服挑战，展现了她的成长。文章通过生动的校园语境（如 a six-story building, hallways stretched in four directions）和人物心理描写（如 keep her head above water，one of the major headaches, be left in the dust 等）增加了代入感，突出了 Eva 初入校园时的迷茫与压力。在跑步情节中，文章通过细致的动作和心理描写展现了 Eva 的焦虑与不自信（如 Soon Eva began to breathe hard, with her heart pounding and legs shaking.），以及她如何通过拆解目标、专注于短期目标（如① Instead, she focused on reaching the shadow cast on the track by an oak tree up ahead. ② Then she concentrated on jogging to the spot where the track curved.），逐步克服挑战。

## 二、学情分析

**基本信息：高一学生，班级人数：68 人；平均分；80 分左右，高一第二学期接触读后续写练习。**

| 项目 | 内容 |
| --- | --- |
| 已有基础 | 1. 熟悉记叙文的类型和结构，了解记叙文六大要素和故事山模型<br>2. 能读懂读后续写所给文本的大意，能准确找出文本中的 who, when, where 等显性信息<br>3. 能根据读后续写所给文本及续写段首提示句，简单完成续写任务<br>4. 会用动词、形容词、副词等进行动作、情绪和心理状态的简单描写 |
| 存在障碍 | 1. 不能准确概括故事内容，续写内容新增原文以外的角色，导致内容与原文缺乏协同性<br>2. 忽略原文语篇结构与语言特色，续写内容中式思维严重、高级复杂词汇堆积，语法结构单一，段落逻辑衔接差等，导致语言风格与原文缺乏协同性<br>3. 不能从深层次理解作者的写作意图，导致主题升华与原文缺乏协同性<br>4. 不能在具体情境中从动作描写、心理描写、环境描写、语言描写等角度完成续写任务<br>5. 不能有效修改续写内容，并提升润色 |
| 发展需求 | 1. 提高语篇的分析能力，准确挖掘文本内容，确保续写内容与原文内容的协同性<br>2. 准确把握语篇结构与语言特征，准确选择词汇、语法结构和恰当的逻辑衔接手段，确保续写语言与原文的协同性<br>3. 学会准确辨别作者的写作意图，正确归纳、提炼语篇所反映的情感、态度和价值观<br>4. 能针对不同场景、精准描写动作、情绪、心理和环境等内容，并积累相关语料<br>5. 了解评分标准，并根据评分标准自行修改、润色 |
| 解决措施 | 1. 借助六何分析法进行语篇分析，快速把握故事核心要素<br>2. 借助故事山梳理故事情节和情感两条线，精准把握故事走向<br>3. 借助五五拍戏教学法，构建续写框架，并设置丰富的故事情节<br>4. 借助点线面润色升级法和连句成篇技巧，提升语言表达和句与句间的逻辑关系，分类积累相关语言表达<br>5. 借助评价标准和“三要六不要”原则，润色习作，提高续写质量 |

## 三、教学目标

通过本节课，学生能够：

**语言能力**

1. 通过面部表情、行为动作和心理活动等多角度描写人物的焦虑与恐惧情绪，提升人物刻画的细腻度。

2. 运用点线面润色升级法，通过细节和情感的描写增强语言表达的丰富性。

**文化意识**

通过分析 Eva 在适应高中的学习生活过程中遇到的困难和挑战，学会运用积极心态应对新环境中的困境。

**思维品质**

1. 运用六何分析法，理解文本的深层含义及其叙事结构，培养批判性思维和逻辑推理能力。

2. 运用五五拍戏教学法，构建清晰的故事框架，培养逻辑思维与创造性思维能力。

**学习能力**

1. 运用心理暗示和设定小目标的技巧，帮助自己在面对挑战时分解任务、克服焦虑和恐惧，提高自我调节能力。

2. 在自评和同伴互评中，培养独立思考与合作学习的能力，提高探究精神和自主学习的意识。

## 四、教学思路

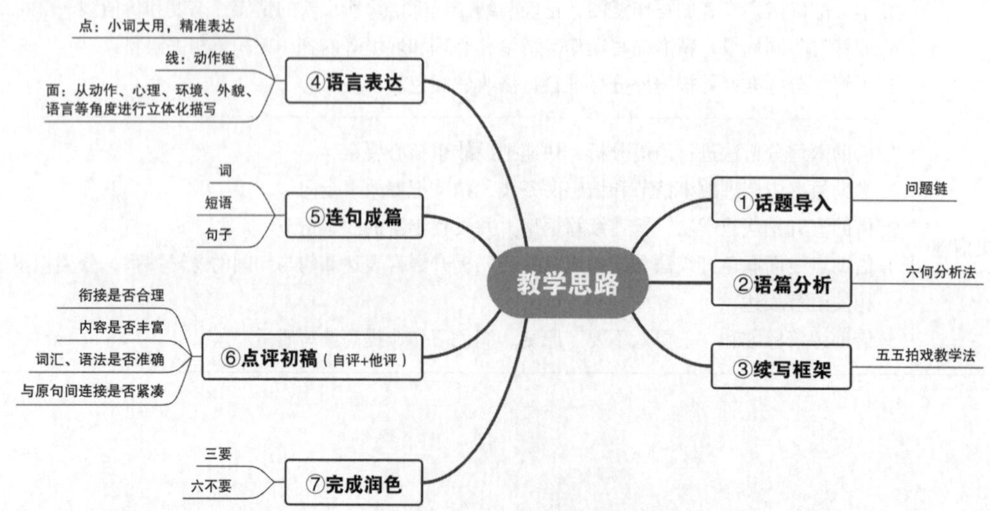

## 五、教学过程

<table>
<tr><th>阶段</th><th>活动形式及步骤</th><th>问题链</th><th>设计意图</th></tr>
<tr><td>话题导入</td><td>1. 话题热身：初入高中校园，你是否遇到过一些让你感到困扰或者焦虑的校园挑战？你是如何应对的？<br>2. 情境创设：假如你面临一个看似无法完成的任务（比如一项学科考试，或者一项体育比赛），你会如何调整自己的情绪，并一步步完成这个任务？</td><td>1. What was the biggest challenge you faced when you first entered high school? Why?<br>2. How did these challenges affect your emotions? Did you feel anxious, confused, or pressured?<br>3. What measures did you take to overcome these challenges?<br>4. When facing difficulties, did you set small goals? Has this approach been effective for you?</td><td>引导学生回顾自身经历，激发共鸣</td></tr>
<tr><td rowspan="2">语篇分析</td><td>1. 快速浏览文章，按照六何分析法提取文本浅层信息（when/where/who）<br><br>**语篇分析**<br>① Eva spent the first week of high school trying to keep her head above water. One of the major headaches for her was finding her way in the huge school building.<br>③ In her first P.E. class, Eva was shocked when Coach Pitt announced that everyone had to run one mile around the track outside.<br><br>**六何分析法**<br>when: the first week of high school; in the first P.E. class<br>where: in the school building; around the track outside<br>who: Eva & Coach Pitt<br>what: story mountain<br>how: analyze the narrative perspective and style<br>why: analyze the purpose</td><td>1. When did the story take place?<br>2. Where did the story take place?<br>3. Who were the key characters in the text?</td><td>运用六何分析法，快速提取文本的浅层信息，了解文章大意</td></tr>
<tr><td>2. 借助故事山梳理文本的情节线和情感线（what）<br><br>**情节分析——story mountain【what】**<br>Para. 1:<br>• Eva met lots of headaches in the first week of high school, one of which was to find right directions in the huge school building.<br>• Eva: upset and anxious<br>Para. 2:<br>• Having a poor sense of direction, Eva decided that she would memorize where her classes were and then pretended that the rest of the places didn't exist.<br>• Eva: frustrated<br>Para. 3–4:<br>• In her first P.E. class, Eva was shocked when Coach Pitt announced that everyone had to run one mile .There was nothing she feared more than having to run a whole mile. She thought. "I'll come in last for sure."<br>• Eva: panicked ,fearful and unconfident<br>Para. 5:<br>• Eva started using a mind trick. She focused on reaching the shadow east on the track by an oak tree up ahead. Then she concentrated on jogging to the spot where the track curved.<br>• Eva: hopeful<br>续写：<br>• Eva succeeded running one mile. D.d she succeed memorizing the right directions of the school building by using mind trick?<br>• Eva: surprised and thrilled, successful?</td><td>1. What was the beginning of the story?<br>2. How did the story develop?<br>3. What was the main conflict of the story?<br>4. What was the solution of the conflict?<br>5. What was the ending of the story?<br>6. What was the reaction of Eva after running one mile successfully ?<br>7. Did Eva succeed in memorizing the directions of the school building by employing her mind trick?</td><td>运用故事山梳理文本的情节、情感两条线，引导学生关注故事走向和人物的情感变化</td></tr>
</table>

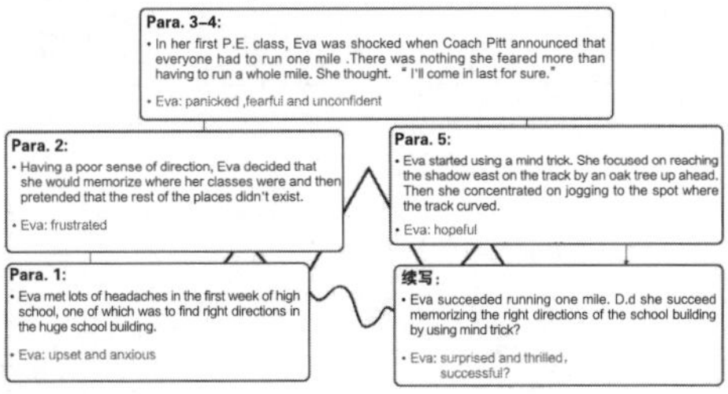

续表

| 阶段 | 活动形式及步骤 | 问题链 | 设计意图 |
| --- | --- | --- | --- |
| 语篇分析 | 3. 标记出文本中有关主人公的描写和介绍，进行人物分析 (who)<br>**人物分析【who】**<br>Eva<br>• Eva spent the first week of high school trying to keep her head above water.<br>• Having a poor sense of direction, She found it impossible to get around in such a huge building.<br>• There was nothing she feared more than having to run a whole mile.<br>• Instead, she focused on reaching the shadow cast on the track by an oak tree up ahead.<br>**Eva was upset, anxious, fearful and unconfident but she was also smart, strategic and determined.**<br>Coach Pitt<br>• In her first P.E. class, Eva was shocked when Coach Pitt announced that everyone had to run one mile around the track outside.<br>• When Coach Pitt said "Nice work!" to her at the finish line...<br>**Coach Pitt was strict but supportive and encouraging.** | 1. Which sentences can show the characters' personalities?<br>2. Can you summarize the characters' personalities? | 通过查找文本中主要人物的所做、所思、所想，引导学生剖析人物性格、推断情感变化，为续写做好准备 |
| 语篇分析 | 4. 分析叙述视角和语言风格（how）<br>**叙述视角与语言风格分析【how】**<br>Narrative perspective<br>• Eva spent the first week of high school trying to keep her head above water.<br>• Having a poor sense of direction, Eva found it impossible to get around in such a huge building.<br>• When Coach Pitt blew his whistle , Eva figured she would be left in the dust.<br>**第三人称视角：Eva/Coach Pitt**<br>Narrative style<br>• One of the major headaches for her was finding her way in the huge school building.<br>• Soon Eva began to breathe hard, with her heart pounding and legs shaking.<br>• "It's just the beginning," she thought. "I'll come in last for sure."<br>**语言风格：simple,clear, descriptive, inner monologue(内心独白)** | 1. What is the narrative perspective of this story?<br>2. What is the narrative style of this story? | 鼓励学生充分研读文本，从叙述角度和写作技巧等层面进行鉴赏，并在续写中大胆模仿，做到语言协同 |
| | 5. 分析文本的情感、态度和价值观 (why)<br>**情感、态度、价值观分析【why】**<br>人与自我<br>By using effective strategies, facing challenges with courage, and steadily working towards our goals, we can overcome difficulties and grow stronger. | What values do you think the author wants to convey to readers through the story? | 引导学生深入思考故事主人公 Eva 如何应对学校生活中的挑战，并成功克服困难，进一步理解作者的意图 |

续表

| 阶段 | 活动形式及步骤 | 问题链 | 设计意图 |
|---|---|---|---|
| 续写框架 | 使用五五拍戏教学法构建一个续写框架（每个段落都续写五个句子，两段续写句子的编号为1—10），并结合情节进行续写，从承上启下、故事结局和情感、态度和价值观等角度，提供拍戏建议<br>Tip 1：确定演员<br>Tip 2：确定出场顺序 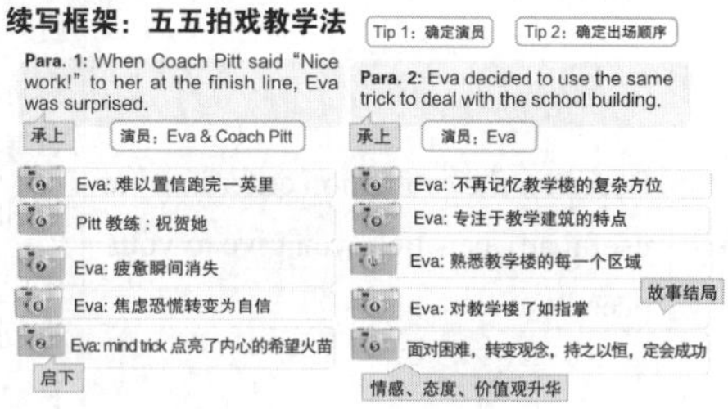<br>**续写框架：五五拍戏教学法**<br>Tip 1：确定演员　Tip 2：确定出场顺序<br>**Para. 1:** When Coach Pitt said "Nice work!" to her at the finish line, Eva was surprised.<br>承上　演员：Eva & Coach Pitt<br>Eva: 难以置信跑完一英里<br>Pitt 教练：祝贺她<br>Eva: 疲惫瞬间消失<br>Eva: 焦虑恐慌转变为自信<br>Eva: mind trick 点亮了内心的希望火苗<br>启下<br>**Para. 2:** Eva decided to use the same trick to deal with the school building.<br>承上　演员：Eva<br>Eva: 不再记忆教学楼的复杂方位<br>Eva: 专注于教学建筑的特点<br>Eva: 熟悉教学楼的每一个区域<br>Eva: 对教学楼了如指掌　故事结局<br>面对困难，转变观念，持之以恒，定会成功<br>情感、态度、价值观升华 | Part 1: What were the main characters in Para.1 and 2?<br>Part 2: 1. Why did Eva feel surprised?<br>2. Why did Eva want to use the same trick to deal with the school building?<br>3. What would Eva do to deal with the school building by using the same mind trick?<br>4. What was the ending of the story?<br>5. What values does the story convey?<br>6. What would Eva's coach do?<br>7. What was the reaction of Eva after getting her coach's approval?<br>8. What changes occurred in Eva's emotions?<br>9. What did Eva specially do to solve the problem of her poor sense of direction?<br>10. Did Eva make any progress in finding the right places? | 提供清晰的续写框架（五五拍戏教学法），引导学生构建合理的故事情节 |
| 语言表达 | 1. 结合续写框架，撰写十句草稿 <br>**续写框架：五五拍戏教学法**<br>**Para. 1:** When Coach Pitt said "Nice work!" to her at the finish line, Eva was surprised.<br>Eva: 难以置信跑完一英里 • She couldn't believe she successfully finished one mile.<br>Pitt 教练：祝贺她 • Her coach Pitt congratulated her.<br>Eva: 疲惫瞬间消失 • Eva's tiredness immediately disappeared.<br>Eva: 焦虑恐慌转变为自信 • Her anxiety and fear turned into confidence.<br>Eva: mind trick 点亮了内心的希望火苗 • Mind trick lighted a fire of hope in Eva's heart.<br>2. 借助点线面润色升级法润色草稿，并标记微场景 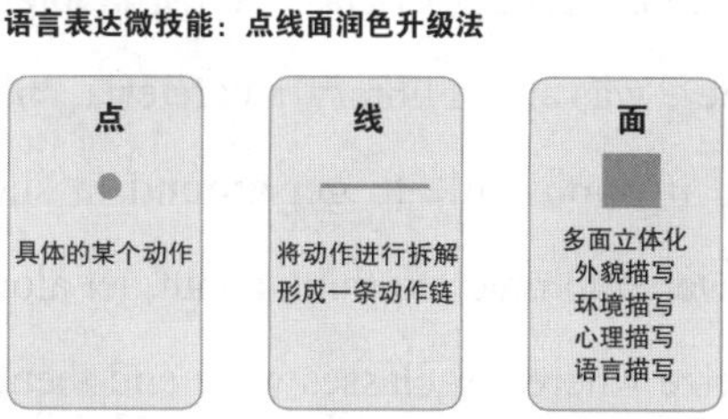 <br>**语言表达微技能：点线面润色升级法**<br>点：具体的某个动作<br>线：将动作进行拆解形成一条动作链<br>面：多面立体化 外貌描写 环境描写 心理描写 语言描写<br>**语言表达：升级表达（微场景＋公式技巧）**<br>**Para.1:** When Coach Pitt said "Nice work!" to her at the finish line, Eva was surprised.<br>【微场景：表达想法】面：心理描写（俚语表达）<br>She couldn't believe she successfully ran one mile.<br>Successfully running one mile was beyond her wildest dreams.<br>【微场景：表扬学生】点：精细化词汇 面：外貌，动作，语言描写<br>Her coach Pitt congratulated her.<br>With a satisfied smile, her coach quickly came over, gave her a big thumbs-up, and praised, "Well done!" | 1. How would you polish your draft?<br>2. Could you summarize the tips to polish your writing? | 通过点线面润色升级法，帮助学生提高写作表达水平，使表达更加精准丰富 |

续表

| 阶段 | 活动形式及步骤 | 问题链 | 设计意图 |
| --- | --- | --- | --- |
| 连句成篇 | 以“词→短语→句子”循序渐进的方式将润色的十句话连句成篇，从而完成初稿<br>**连句成篇**<br>**请注意连接成分，并进行分类。**<br>连接成分：词 ③④；短语 ①②⑤；句子 ⑥<br>***Paragraph 1:*** *When Coach Pitt said “Nice work!” to her at the finish line, Eva was surprised.* Successfully running one mile was beyond her wildest dreams. ① At the same time, with a satisfied smile, her coach quickly came over, gave a big thumbs-up, and praised, "Well done!" ② Upon hearing that, Eva's exhaustion instantly disappeared and she leapt to her feet in great excitement. ③ Suddenly, her previous anxiety and fear gave way to the newfound self-confidence. It was at this very moment that the mind trick lighted a flame of hope in her.<br>***Paragraph 2:*** *Eva decided to use the same trick to deal with the school building.* No longer did she struggle to memorize the complicated directions. ④ Instead, she fixed her mind on their distinctive features: classrooms marked with blue doors, the book- shaped entrance of the library and mouth-watering smell from the cafe. ⑤ Each day passing by, Eva began to get herself familiar with every area. What had been a headache became as familiar as the back of her hand. ⑥ As she looked back, Eva firmly believed that changing our mindset and facing challenges with determination is the key to achieving our goals. | How do you put the following sentences together? | 运用词、短语和从句，使语言衔接更加有序 |
| 点评初稿 | 结合“读后续写评价标准”及“读后续写自评互评表”进行自评和互评【详见附录一和附录二】 | Based on the evaluation criteria, what useful advice would you give to your peers? | 提供详细的评分标准及三个重要的写作要点和六个写作陷阱，使学生在创作时更具针对性，牢记评价要点 |
| 润色习作 | 结合评价反馈润色自己的习作 | How could you refine your writing based on the feedback? | 结合同伴反馈，润色并完善写作内容 |

## 附录 1：真题文本

① Eva spent the first week of high school trying to keep her head above water. One of the major headaches for her was finding her way in the huge school building. It was a six-story building. On each floor, hallways stretched in four directions, leading to classrooms, laboratories, and teachers' offices. Somewhere in the building, there was also a library, a cafeteria, and a gym.

② Having a poor sense of direction, Eva found it impossible to get around in such a huge building. All the different hallways and rooms were too much to think about, let alone commit to memory. She decided that she would memorize where her classes were and then pretended that the rest of the places didn't exist.

③ In her first P.E. class, Eva was shocked when Coach Pitt announced that everyone had to run one mile around the track outside. She searched the faces of her classmates for signs of panic. There was nothing she feared more than having to run a whole mile. To Eva, “a mile” was used to describe long distances. It was ten miles from her home to her grandfather's, and that always seemed like a long way, even in a car!

④ When Coach Pitt blew his whistle, Eva figured she would be left in the dust. However, while some of her classmates edged ahead, others actually fell behind. "It's just the beginning," she thought. "I'll come in last for sure."

⑤ Soon Eva began to breathe hard, with her heart pounding and legs shaking. Feeling desperate, Eva started using a mind trick on herself. She stopped thinking about the word "mile." Instead, she focused on reaching the shadow cast on the track by an oak tree up ahead. Then she concentrated on jogging to the spot where the track curved (拐弯). After that, she tried to see if she could complete her first lap. One lap turned into two, then three, then four.

注意

1. 续写词数应为 150 个左右；
2. 请按如下格式在答题卡的相应位置作答。

When Coach Pitt said "Great work" to her at the finish line, Eva was surprised. ___________

______________________________________________________________________

Eva decided to use the same trick to deal with the school building. ___________________

______________________________________________________________________

附录 2：参考范文

**When Coach Pitt said "Great work" to her at the finish line, Eva was surprised.** Successfully running one mile was beyond her wildest dreams. At the same time, with a satisfied smile, her coach quickly came over, gave her a big thumbs-up, and praised, "Well done!" Upon hearing that, Eva's exhaustion instantly disappeared and she leapt to her feet in great excitement. Suddenly, her previous anxiety and fear gave way to the newfound self-confidence. It was at this very moment that the mind trick lighted a flame of hope in her.

**Eva decided to use the same trick to deal with the school building.** No longer did she struggle to memorize the complicated directions. Instead, she fixed her mind on their distinctive features: classrooms marked with blue doors, the book-shaped entrance of the library and mouth-watering smell from the cafe. Each day passing by, Eva began to get herself familiar with every area. What had been a headache became as familiar as the back of her hand. As she looked back, Eva firmly believed that changing our mindset and facing challenges with determination is the key to achieving our goals.

# 第二节

# 以 2023 年新高考 I、II 卷为例的读后续写教学设计案例

## 一、文本分析

**What** 本文的主题语境是“人与自我”，涉及“认识自我、丰富自我、完善自我”的内容。故事讲述了“我”——一名移民美国的巴西中学生最初因英语非其母语，对写作产生抗拒情绪。通过教师的鼓励和自己的努力，“我”逐渐克服了对写作的恐惧和疑虑，最终发现写作的乐趣，并在比赛中取得不错的成绩。

续写第一段的段首句：几周后，当“我”差点忘了这个比赛的时候，比赛结果传来了。

续写第二段的段首句：颁奖典礼结束后，“我”去了教师的办公室。

综上所述，故事的走向可能是“我”在写作比赛中获得了不错的名次，并在获奖后当面感谢教师的鼓励与指导。

**Why** 本文通过分享“我”参加写作比赛的心路历程，展现了面对困难时的坚持与成长。同时，文章也突出了教师在挖掘学生潜力，鼓励学生克服挑战，帮助学生重建自信中扮演着不可或缺的角色。文章最终传达了一种乐观和积极的生活态度，即使面对潜在的失败，也应勇于尝试并进行自我挑战，从中可能发现新的热情和个人价值。

**How** 本文以第一人称的视角，采用了记叙文常见的“conflict-solution”模式，讲述了对于写作，“我”从排斥到接受，从困惑到收获的转变过程。文章使用幽默的语言和有趣的情节表达所面临的挑战和困难。例如，通过将“我”与 Paul Revere 的马进行比喻，巧妙地表达了自己在写作过程中的感受。文章通过设问（如 Did he get tired? Have doubts? Did he want to quit?），引导读者思考，增强了文章的互动性和思考深度。

同时，文章多处采用了排比的修辞手法（①I got tired. I had doubts. I wanted to quit.

② I kept going. I worked hard. I checked my spelling. ③ I asked my older sister to correct my grammar. I checked out a half-dozen books on Paul Revere from the library. I even read a few of them.），增强了文章的感染力。

## 二、学情分析

**基本信息：高二学生，班级人数：56 人；平均分：95 分左右；读后续写平均分：16 分。**

| 项目 | 内容 |
| --- | --- |
| 已有基础 | 1. 能够快速梳理出 who, when, where 等浅层信息<br>2. 能够用自己的话概括出文章大意 what<br>3. 能够从 why 出发，挖掘作者的写作意图<br>4. 会利用五五拍戏教学法，合理衔接开头句，续写内容较丰富<br>5. 了解该题型得分要点 |
| 存在障碍 | 1. 缺乏对文章细节的把握，找不到续写的关键线索<br>2. 缺乏对文章叙述角度 how 的认知，导致续写语言风格不协同<br>3. 语言表达不地道，错误使用词汇、语法，影响意义的表达<br>4. 较少使用连接成分，导致续写内容缺乏连贯性 |
| 发展需求 | 1. 学会挖掘文章中的关键线索<br>2. 学会分析文章的叙述风格，赏析好词好句，提升语言表达<br>3. 学会合理连接句间逻辑关系 |
| 解决措施 | 1. 以“conflict-solution”模式，梳理故事的情节和情感两条线，精准挖掘续写的关键线索<br>2. 运用“点→线→面”升级思路，多角度提升语言表达能力<br>3. 借助“词→短语→句子”技巧，探索连句成篇新思路 |

## 三、教学目标

通过本节课，学生能够：

**语言能力**

1. 理解并使用 apply oneself, have a good shot, give it a try 等鼓励性表述，增强续写内容语言的表现力。

2. 赏析并模仿原文中的排比结构。增强续写内容的节奏感和感染力。

**文化意识**

理解面对困难时应保持积极的态度，并努力克服困难，同时也要珍惜并感谢他人的帮助与支持。

**思维品质**

1. 通过分析人物内心变化，理解故事中的冲突和解决过程，培养批判性思维和问题解决能力。

2. 从情节发展中提炼出关键线索，进行推理和预测，提升逻辑思维能力。

3. 通过构建合理的续写框架，确保故事结构的清晰和条理性，培养系统思维能力。

**学习能力**

在分析和续写过程中，灵活运用不同的写作技巧，提升语言表达的多样性。

## 四、教学思路

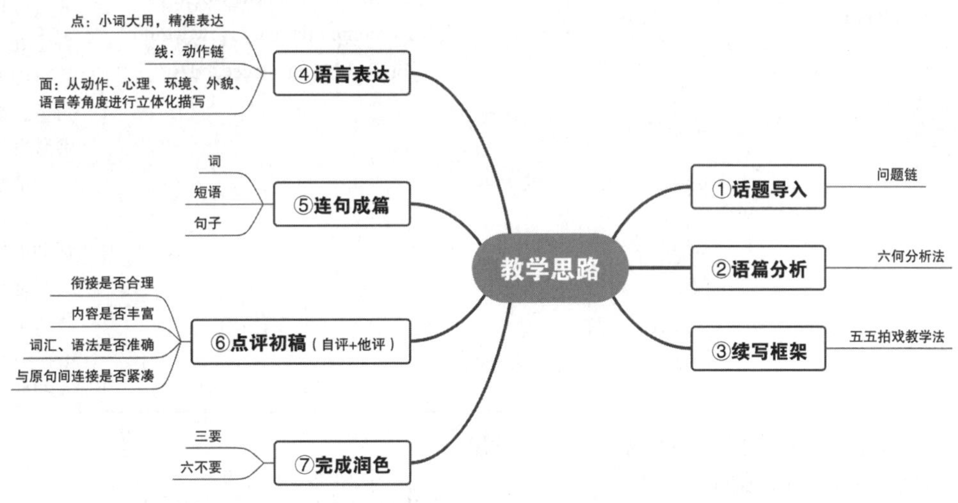

## 五、教学过程

<table>
<tr><th>阶段</th><th>活动形式及步骤</th><th>问题链</th><th>设计意图</th></tr>
<tr><td>话题导入</td><td>1. 话题热身：你是否在英语写作上遇到过困难？你是如何克服这些困难的？<br>2. 情境创设：想象你需要参加一个写作比赛，但你一直对写作充满恐惧和不自信。你会如何克服这种恐惧？如果你最终成功了，你会有什么样的感受？</td><td>1. Have you ever faced difficulties in English writing?<br>2. How did you overcome them?<br>3. Imagine you were about to enter a writing contest, but you were terrified and lacked confidence in your writing, how would you overcome this fear? How would you feel if you succeeded?</td><td>1. 能激发学生对自己写作经历的回顾，并让他们反思克服困难的过程<br>2. 通过换位思考的方式帮助学生感受“写作恐惧”和“自信重建”这一情感转变。设想自己处于故事中的角色，能够激发学生的情感共鸣，并帮助他们更好地理解文本中的情节和人物变化</td></tr>
<tr><td>语篇分析</td><td>1. 快速浏览文章，按照六何分析法提取文章浅层信息（when/where/who）<br>语篇分析<br>① When I was in middle school, my social studies teacher asked me to enter a writing contest, I said no without thinking. I did not love writing. My family came from Brazil, so English was only my second language. Writing was so difficult and painful for me that my teacher had allowed me to present my paper on the sinking of the Titanic by acting out a play, where I played all the parts. No one laughed harder than he did.<br>
<table>
<tr><th colspan="4">六何分析法</th></tr>
<tr><td>when</td><td>when I was in middle school</td><td>what</td><td>Story mountain</td></tr>
<tr><td>where</td><td>in middle school</td><td>how</td><td>analyze the narrative perspective and style</td></tr>
<tr><td>who</td><td>I ; my social studies teacher</td><td>why</td><td>analyze the purpose</td></tr>
</table></td><td>1. When did the story take place?<br>2. Where did the story take place?<br>3. Who were the key characters in the text?<br>4. What happened in the story?<br>5. Why did the story happen?</td><td>运用六何分析法，梳理语篇的构成要素</td></tr>
</table>

续表

| 阶段 | 活动形式及步骤 | 问题链 | 设计意图 |
| --- | --- | --- | --- |
| | 2. 借助故事山梳理文本的情节线和情感线（what） 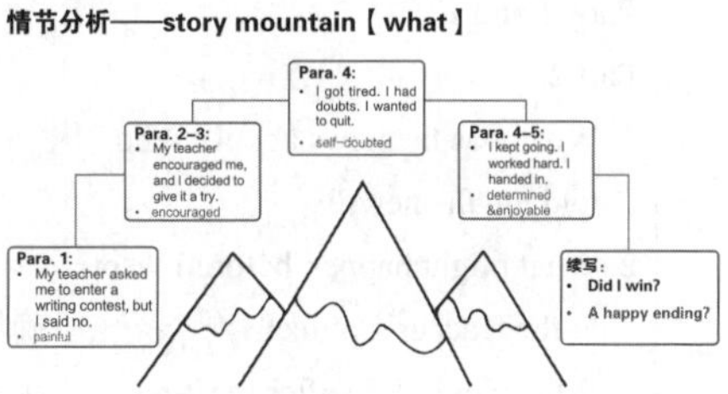<br>**情节分析——story mountain【what】**<br>Para. 1:<br>• My teacher asked me to enter a writing contest, but I said no.<br>• painful<br>Para. 2–3:<br>• My teacher encouraged me, and I decided to give it a try.<br>• encouraged<br>Para. 4:<br>• I got tired. I had doubts. I wanted to quit.<br>• self-doubted<br>Para. 4–5:<br>• I kept going. I worked hard. I handed in.<br>• determined &enjoyable<br>续写：<br>• Did I win?<br>• A happy ending? | 1. What was the beginning of the story?<br>2. How did the story develop?<br>3. What was the main conflict of the story?<br>4. What was the resolution of the conflict?<br>5. What might be the ending of the story?<br>6. How did my feelings change? | 运用故事山梳理文本的情节、情感两条线，引导学生关注故事走向和情感变化 |
| | 3. 标记出文本中有关主人公的描写和介绍，进行人物分析 (who) 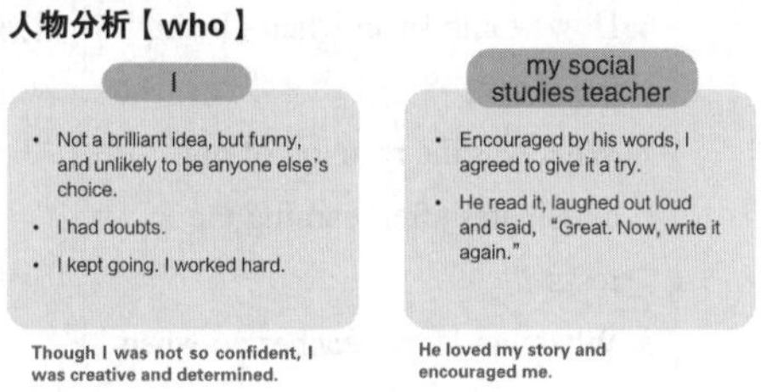<br>**人物分析【who】**<br>I<br>• Not a brilliant idea, but funny, and unlikely to be anyone else's choice.<br>• I had doubts.<br>• I kept going. I worked hard.<br>**Though I was not so confident, I was creative and determined.**<br>my social studies teacher<br>• Encouraged by his words, I agreed to give it a try.<br>• He read it, laughed out loud and said, "Great. Now, write it again."<br>**He loved my story and encouraged me.** | 1. Which sentences can show the characters' personalities?<br>2. Could you conclude the characters' personalities? | 关注故事主要人物的描写并分析，确保续写故事走向不偏离人物特征 |
| 语篇分析 | 4. 分析叙述视角与语言风格（how） 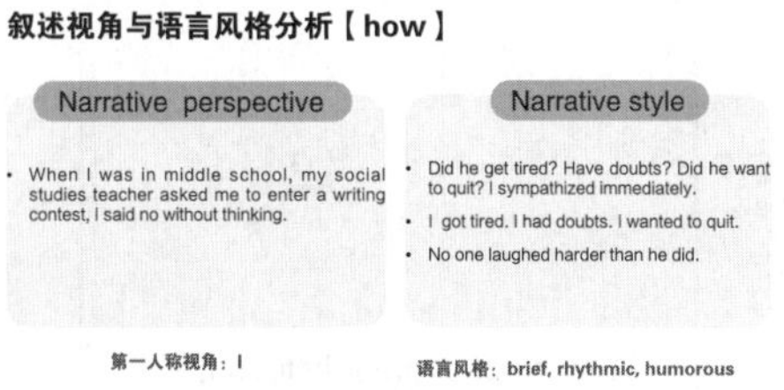<br>**叙述视角与语言风格分析【how】**<br>Narrative perspective<br>• When I was in middle school, my social studies teacher asked me to enter a writing contest, I said no without thinking.<br>**第一人称视角：I**<br>Narrative style<br>• Did he get tired? Have doubts? Did he want to quit? I sympathized immediately.<br>• I got tired. I had doubts. I wanted to quit.<br>• No one laughed harder than he did.<br>**语言风格：brief, rhythmic, humorous** | What are the narrative perspective and narrative style of this article? | 关注故事的叙述视角和风格，确保续写风格与原文保持协同 |
| | 5. 提炼分析文本的情感、态度、价值观 (why) <br>**情感、态度、价值观分析【why】**<br>人与人<br>We should never forget those who have ever helped us.<br>人与自我<br>Never let self-doubt define our life. | 1. What would "I" say in the award presentation?<br>2. What values or life perspectives do you think the author wants to convey to readers through the story? | 引导学生深入思考故事中蕴含的情感、态度及价值观，进一步理解作者的意图 |

续表

| 阶段 | 活动形式及步骤 | 问题链 | 设计意图 |
|---|---|---|---|
| 续写框架 | 使用五五拍戏教学法构建一个续写框架：<br>Tip 1：确定演员<br>Tip 2：确定出场顺序<br>Tip 3：戏份不够，细节或环境来凑 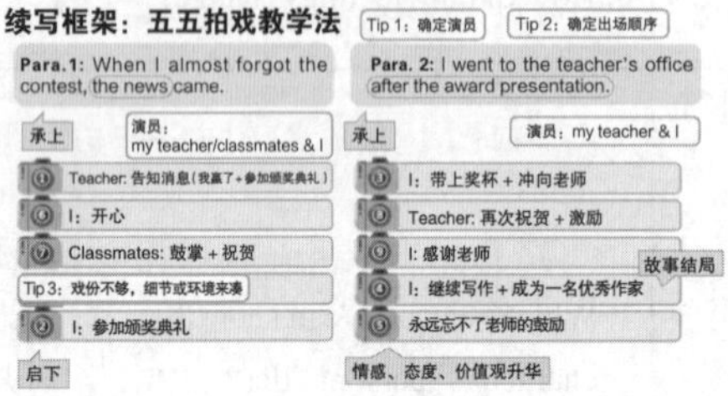<br>续写框架：五五拍戏教学法<br>Tip 1：确定演员 Tip 2：确定出场顺序<br>Para.1: When I almost forgot the contest, the news came.<br>承上 演员：my teacher/classmates & I<br>Teacher: 告知消息（我赢了+参加颁奖典礼）<br>I：开心<br>Classmates: 鼓掌+祝贺<br>Tip 3：戏份不够，细节或环境来凑<br>I：参加颁奖典礼<br>启下<br>Para. 2: I went to the teacher's office after the award presentation.<br>承上 演员：my teacher & I<br>I：带上奖杯+冲向老师<br>Teacher: 再次祝贺+激励<br>I: 感谢老师<br>I：继续写作+成为一名优秀作家<br>永远忘不了老师的鼓励<br>故事结局<br>情感、态度、价值观升华 | Part 1:<br>What were the main characters in Para. 1 and 2?<br>Part 2:<br>1. What was the news about? Who told me the news?<br>2. What might happen before I went to the teacher's office?<br>3. What would I do after meeting the teacher?<br>4. What was the ending of the story?<br>5. What values or life lessons does the story convey?<br>6. How would I feel when I heard the news?<br>7. What was the reaction of my classmates after learning the result?<br>8. What would the teacher do when he saw the trophy in my hand?<br>9. How could I express my gratitude to the teacher? | 确保学生在续写时拥有清晰的思路，合理构建故事情节，同时关注人物情感和价值观的表达 |
| 语言表达 | 1. 结合续写框架，撰写草稿 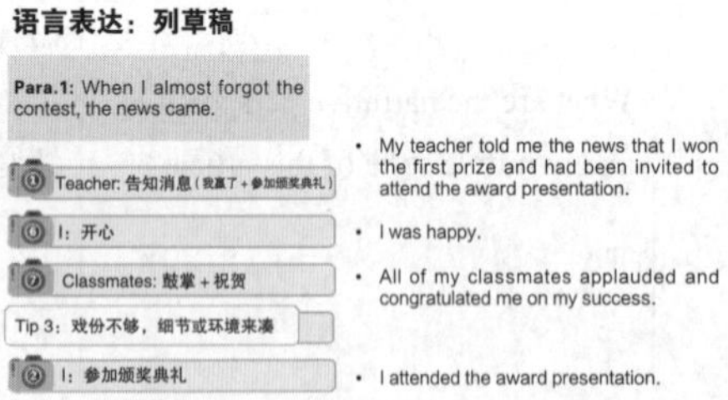<br>语言表达：列草稿<br>Para.1: When I almost forgot the contest, the news came.<br>Teacher: 告知消息（我赢了+参加颁奖典礼） • My teacher told me the news that I won the first prize and had been invited to attend the award presentation.<br>I：开心 • I was happy.<br>Classmates: 鼓掌+祝贺 • All of my classmates applauded and congratulated me on my success.<br>Tip 3：戏份不够，细节或环境来凑<br>I：参加颁奖典礼 • I attended the award presentation.<br>2. 教师示范讲解点线面润色升级法，并进行对应的微技能训练<br>语言表达微技能：点线面润色升级法 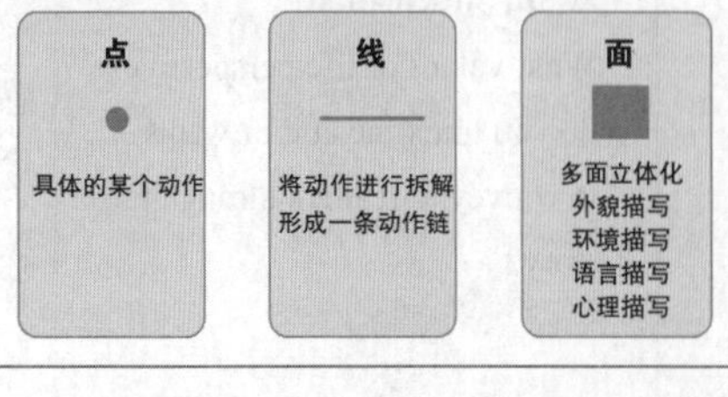<br>点：具体的某个动作<br>线：将动作进行拆解 形成一条动作链<br>面：多面立体化 外貌描写 环境描写 语言描写 心理描写 | 1. How would you polish your draft?<br>2. Could you conclude the tips to polish your writing? | |

续表

| 阶段 | 活动形式及步骤 | 问题链 | 设计意图 |
| --- | --- | --- | --- |
| 语言表达 | 3. 润色草稿，并梳理升级思路<br>**语言表达：升级表达**<br>【微场景：表示祝贺】<br>点：精准化用词<br>面：环境描写<br>All of my classmates applauded and congratulated me on my success.<br>In the cheerful atmosphere of the classroom, every one of my classmates burst into applause and offered their congratulations on my success.<br>【微场景：参加颁奖典礼】<br>线：动作链<br>句式升级：排比句（语言协同）<br>I attended the award presentation.<br>The moment I stepped on the stage, I was greeted by a familiar broad smile from my social studies teacher. In that moment, all the self-doubt disappeared. All my previous hard work paid off. And all I wanted was to visit him. |  | 通过使用点线面润色升级法，帮助学生提高写作水平，使表达更加精准、丰富 |
| 连句成篇 | 以“词→短语→句子”循序渐进的方式将通过以上环节润色的十句话进行连句成篇，从而完成初稿<br>**连句成篇**<br>**请注意连接成分，并进行分类。**<br>连接成分：副词 ②；短语 ①⑤⑥⑦⑧⑨；句子 ③④<br>***Paragraph 1***: When I almost forgot the contest, the news came. I won the first prize! And there would be an award presentation in two days! ① Upon hearing the result, I felt on the top of the world. ② Meanwhile, in the cheerful atmosphere of the classroom, every one of my classmates burst into applause and offered their congratulations on my success. ③ Soon the big day arrived. ④ The moment I stepped on the stage, I was greeted by a familiar smile from my social studies teacher. ⑤ In that moment, all the self-doubt disappeared. All my previous hard work paid off. And all I wanted was to visit him.<br>***Paragraph 2***: I went to the teacher's office after the award presentation. ⑥ With the trophy in hand, I stepped forward with eagerness, ready to throw my arms around him. ⑦ Noticing my approach, he looked up, gestured with a thumbs-up and praised, “Congratulations! I always know that writing is in your blood!” ⑧ Driven by his words, I smiled through tears of gratitude and said, saying "Without your encouragement, I might never find a writer inside me.” ⑨ Now, many years have passed and I have written more than ten bestsellers, during which my teacher's belief in me always serves as the fuel that keeps me going. | How do you put the above sentences together smoothly and coherently? | 运用“词→短语→句子”的方法，使语言衔接更加有序 |
| 点评初稿 | 结合“读后续写评价标准”及“读后续写自评互评表”进行自评和互评【详见附录一和附录二】 | Based on the evaluation criteria, what useful advice would you give to your partner? | 提供详细的评分标准及“三要六不要”原则，使学生在写作时更具针对性，牢记评价要点 |
| 润色习作 | 结合评价反馈润色自己的习作 | How could you refine your writing based on the feedback? | 结合同伴反馈，润色并完善写作内容 |

## 附录 1：真题文本

① When I was in middle school, my social studies teacher asked me to enter a writing contest. I said no without thinking. I did not love writing. My family came from Brazil, so English was only my second language. Writing was so difficult and painful for me that my teacher had allowed me to present my paper on the sinking of the Titanic by acting out a play, where I played all the parts. No one laughed harder than he did.

② So, why did he suddenly force me to do something at which I was sure to fail? His reply: "Because I love your stories. If you're willing to apply yourself, I think you have a good shot at this." Encouraged by his words, I agreed to give it a try.

③ I chose Paul Revere's horse as my subject. Paul Revere was a silversmith (银匠) in Boston who rode a horse at night on April 18, 1775 to Lexington to warn people that British soldiers were coming. My story would come straight from the horse's mouth. Not a brilliant idea, but funny, and unlikely to be anyone else's choice.

④ What did the horse think, as sped through the night? Did he get tired? Have doubts? Did he want to quit? I sympathized immediately. I got tired. I had doubts. I wanted to quit. But, like Revere's horse, I kept going. I worked hard. I checked my spelling. I asked my older sister to correct my grammar. I checked out a half-dozen books on Paul Revere from the library. I even read a few of them.

⑤ When I handed in the essay to my teacher, he read it, laughed out loud and said, "Great. Now, write it again." I wrote it again, and again and again. When I finally finished it, the thought of winning had given way to the enjoyment of writing. If I didn't win, I wouldn't care.

**注意**

1. 续写词数应为 150 个左右；
2. 请按如下格式在答题卡的相应位置作答。

A few weeks later, when I almost forgot the contest, there came the news.________________

______________________________________________________________________

I went to my teacher's office after the award presentation.________________________

______________________________________________________________________

附录 2：参考范文

**When I almost forgot the contest, the news came.** I won the first prize! And there would be an award presentation in two days! Upon hearing the result, I felt on the top of the world. Meanwhile, a round of enthusiastic applause from my classmates filled the classroom. Soon the big day arrived. The moment I stepped on the stage, I was greeted by a familiar smile from my social teacher. In that moment, all the self-doubt disappeared. All my previous hard work paid off. And all I wanted was to visit him.

**I went to the teacher's office after the award presentation.** With the trophy in hand, I stepped forward with eagerness, ready to throw my arms around him. Noticing my approach, he looked up, gestured with a thumbs-up and offered a warm praise, "Congratulations! I always know that writing is in your blood!" In spired by his words, I smiled through tears of gratitude and said "Without your encouragement, I might never find a writer inside me." Now, many years have passed and I have written more than ten bestsellers, during which my teacher's belief in me always serves as the fuel that keeps me going.

# 第三节

## 以 2024 届高三第二次学业质量和评价（T8 联考）为例的读后续写教学设计案例

### 一、文本分析

**What** 本文的主题语境是“人与社会”，涉及“遇困脱险类”内容。本文主要描述了一位学生在放学后乘坐电梯回家时，与一位老年邻居一起遭遇了电梯突然下坠并停在第五层的紧急情况。

续写第一段的段首句：几分钟过去了，但是没有人来帮忙。

续写第二段的段首句：“嘭！”当“我”听到电梯门另一侧有消防员的声音时，“我”的希望被重新点燃了。

根据续写两段的段首句内容，可以预测后面的故事情节：被困在电梯里的“我”和 Mrs. Lim 共渡难关，并且等来了消防员的救援。

**Why** 本文通过描述一次遭遇电梯故障的事件，探讨了人们在紧急情况下，面对恐惧和未知时的不同反应，强调了保持冷静、互相扶持及积极应对的重要性。“我”在面对突发状况时，主动安慰并照顾年迈的邻居，体现了对他人的关怀和同理心。文章旨在启发读者思考如何在困境中帮助他人、积极面对挑战，强调人与人之间的互助精神和坚韧品质。

**How** 本文以第一人称的视角按照时间顺序描述了“我”和 Mrs. Lim 遭遇电梯故障的经历。文章语言简洁明了，使用了许多生动的动词和形容词描述电梯下坠的情境和人物的反应，如“the lift fell down increasingly fast”和“loud clanking sounds”等词句，生动地描绘了电梯出故障时的惊险场景；“dragged my feet”（拖着我的脚走）表现心情沉重；“hobbled in”（蹒跚走进）描绘邻居的衰老状态；“icy fear crept up my spine”（冰冷的恐惧爬上我的脊背）形容恐惧。同时，文章运用了一些短句、口语化的表达及直接引语，展现了人物的内心活动和情感状态，增强了文章的表现力，使文章更具真实感和可读性。

## 二、学情分析

**基本信息：高三理科班学生（美术艺术生），平均分：90 分左右；续写平均分：13 分左右。**

| 项目 | 内容 |
|---|---|
| 已有基础 | 1. 熟悉“遇困脱险”类主题语境和相关词汇<br>2. 能够梳理、分析文本的基本信息（who, when, where）<br>3. 能够梳理文本的情节线<br>4. 会考虑情感、态度和价值观的升华<br>5. 基本能够在规定时间内完成续写任务 |
| 存在障碍 | 1. 容易忽略分析人物性格和故事的情感线<br>2. 不能精准挖掘出续写线索，导致续写内容偏离主线<br>3. 表达续写情节的上下句之间不连贯，缺乏逻辑性<br>4. 语言表达能力较弱，存在用词不地道、语法运用不准确等问题 |
| 发展需求 | 1. 学会根据情节线，梳理出主要人物的情感变化<br>2. 学会挖掘文本线索，建构合理、有逻辑的续写情节<br>3. 学会使用连句成篇技巧，提高续写内容的连贯性和衔接性<br>4. 提升语言表达技能，确保续写内容的语言准确、生动 |
| 解决措施 | 1. 借助六何分析法开展语篇分析，精准把握故事的核心要素<br>2. 借助故事山梳理故事的情节和情感两条线，精准把握故事走向<br>3. 借助五五拍戏教学法，构建合理的续写情节和框架<br>4. 借助点线面润色升级法和连句成篇技巧，丰富语言表达，提高语篇的连贯性 |

## 三、教学目标

通过本节课学生能够：

**语言能力**

1. 通过分析文本中的环境描写（The lights on the buttons have gone out.）、心理描写 (It dawned on me that we were trapped.)、动作描写 (come to an abrupt stop, fall down increasingly fast) 和外貌描写 (heart beat hard and fast, hands turn cold and wet with sweat, an icy fear crept up my spine) 等，掌握刻画紧急情况和渲染紧张气氛的语言技巧。

2. 通过分析角色之间的对话和互动，学习如何在叙述中有效使用直接和间接对话描绘人物关系及其心理状态。如：“We will never get out!” She cried with her face pale.

3. 学会使用过渡词和连贯句来增强文章叙述的流畅性和逻辑性。

**文化意识**

1. 通过学习主人公在险境中临危不乱，帮助被困老人的故事，认识在危急时刻保持冷静、积极应对的重要性，提升个人的文明素养和社会责任感。

2. 通过分析电梯老旧状况和对周边环境的描写，思考并讨论城市化进程中社区老化问题及其对居民日常生活的影响。

**思维品质**

1. 学会运用六何分析法梳理人物的行为逻辑和情节发展，以增强逻辑分析能力。

2. 学会运用五五拍戏教学法设计合理且创新的情节发展，培养逻辑推理能力和创造性思维。

3. 通过团体讨论和角色扮演分析故事情节并提出具体的改进方案，提升其批判性思维和创造性思维能力。

**学习能力**

1. 通过模拟以救援为情境的小组活动，培养协作学习和解决问题的能力。

2. 在自评和小组互评的过程中，提升自我反思和批判性分析的能力，并提高自己的语言运用能力。

## 四、教学思路

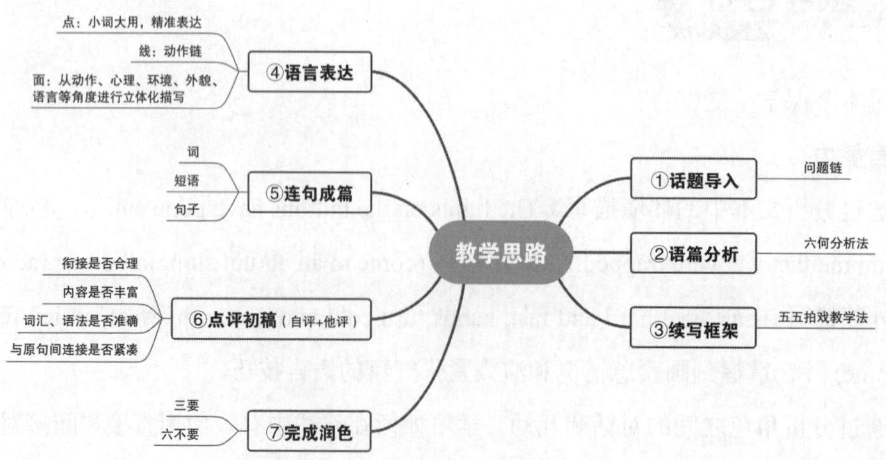

## 五、教学过程

<table>
<tr><th>阶段</th><th>活动形式及步骤</th><th>问题链</th><th>设计意图</th></tr>
<tr><td>话题导入</td><td>头脑风暴：假如你和一位老人被困在电梯中，你将如何应对</td><td>1. What would you do if you were caught in a lift?<br>2. What would you do if you were caught in a lift with an elderly person?</td><td>创设情境，激发学生兴趣，激活学生困境自救常识，为后续阅读做铺垫</td></tr>
<tr><td rowspan="3">语篇分析</td><td>1. 运用六何分析法，梳理文本的浅层信息（who, where, when）<br><br>语篇分析<br>① When we were finally dismissed from the last class of the day, the students streamed out of the classrooms. It was another boring day after school...<br>② The lift lobby（电梯间）of my flat was old and dirty. The walls, which were painted white, had been dirtied over many years. I reached my flat's lobby, and pressed the lift button and went in. Just then, Mrs. Lim, my elderly neighbour, hobbled（蹒跚）in...<br><br>六何分析法<br>when: a boring day after school<br>where: in the lift lobby<br>who: I, Mrs. Lim<br>what: Story mountain<br>how: analyze the narrative perspective and style<br>why: analyze the purpose</td><td>1. When did the story take place?<br>2. Where did the story take place?<br>3. Who were the main characters in the story?</td><td>借助六何分析法梳理文本的基本要素，了解文章的内容</td></tr>
<tr><td>2. 借助故事山梳理文本的情节线和情感线（what）<br><br>情节分析——story mountain【what】<br>Para. 4:<br>• I pressed the buttons hard several times, but it was of no help.<br>• I: panicked, anxious<br>Para. 2–3:<br>• Unfortunately, the lift came to an abrupt stop at the fifth floor.<br>• I: nervous, afraid<br>Para. 4–5:<br>• I attempted to comfort and calm Mrs. Lim.<br>• I: calm, caring<br>Para. 1:<br>• After school, I took the lift, and politely greeted my neighbour Mrs. Lim in the lift lobby.<br>• I: polite<br>续写：<br>• What happened next?<br>• Could Mrs. Lim and I be rescued?<br>• I & Mrs. Lim (potentially) relieved, grateful</td><td>1. What was the beginning of the story?<br>2. How did the story develop?<br>3. What was the main conflict of the story?<br>4. What was the resolution of the conflict?<br>5. What was the ending of the story?<br>6. How did my feelings change?</td><td>借助故事山梳理文本的情节和情感线，引导学生关注故事走向和情感变化</td></tr>
<tr><td>3. 找出与主要人物相关的句子，如语言、动作等，并分析人物的性格（who）<br><br>人物分析【who】<br>I<br>• I held the lift door open, flashing a friendly smile, and politely greeted her. ...She thanked me for being so polite.<br>• I had no time to lose. I tried my very best to comfort her, telling her that everything would be all right and that we needed to find out how to get out safely.<br>I was polite, helpful and responsible, and I could stay calm in face of emergencies.<br><br>Mrs.Lim<br>• Mrs. Lim, my elderly neighbour, hobbled in. She looked ancient with tissue paper white hair, wearing a faded old-fashioned dress.<br>• Mrs. Lim was hysterical.<br>• "We will never get out!" she cried with her face pale...Mrs. Lim burst into tears...Mrs. Lim began having trouble breathing...<br>Mrs. Lim was very old and not in good health. She was timid and emotional.</td><td>1. Which sentences can show the characters' personalities?<br>2. What are the characters' personalities?</td><td>引导学生有意识地分析人物的性格特点，确保续写的故事走向不偏离人物特征</td></tr>
</table>

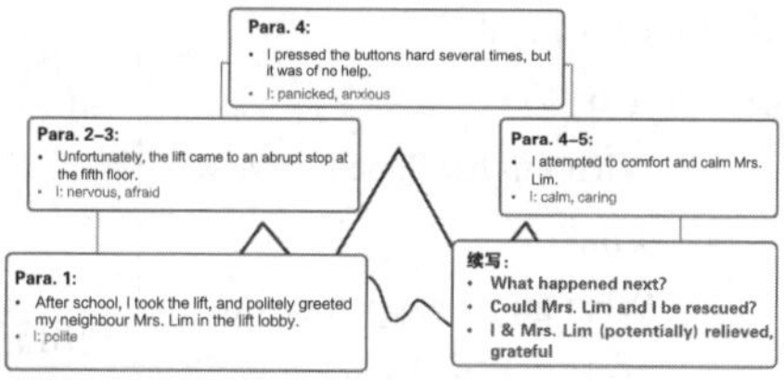

续表

| 阶段 | 活动形式及步骤 | 问题链 | 设计意图 |
| --- | --- | --- | --- |
| 语篇分析 | 4. 分析语篇的叙述视角和语言风格，并找出文本中的相关句子（how）<br>**叙述视角与语言风格分析【how】**<br>Narrative perspective<br>• I dragged my feet home as I sighed.<br>• Just then, Mrs. Lim,... She looked ancient with tissue paper white hair... I asked her how she felt that day and pressed the buttons. She thanked me for being so polite, then we were silent..<br>第一人称视角：I/We<br>Narrative style<br>• When we were finally dismissed from the last class of the day, the students streamed out of the classrooms.<br>• My heart beat hard and fast as my hands turned cold and wet with sweat.<br>• "We will never get out!" she cried with her face pale.<br>语言风格 :descriptive; vivid; conversational; straightforward | 1. What is the narrative perspective of this article?<br>2. What is the narrative style of this article? | 引导学生关注文本的叙述视角和语言风格，确保续写内容的语言与原文协同 |
| | 5. 提炼、分析文本的情感、态度和价值观 (why)<br>**情感态度价值观分析【why】**<br>人与社会<br>Social services and interpersonal communication<br>人与自我<br>Understanding and helping<br>Positive attitudes toward life | What values or life perspectives does the story convey? | 引导学生深入思考故事中蕴含的情感、态度及价值观，进一步理解作者的意图 |
| 续写框架 | 使用五五拍戏教学法构建一个续写框架（每个段落都续写五个句子，两段续写句子的编号为1-10），并结合情节续写，从承上启下、故事结局和情感、态度、价值观等角度，提供拍戏建议。<br>Tip 1：确定演员<br>Tip 2：确定出场顺序<br>Tip 3：戏份不够，细节或环境来凑<br>**续写框架：五五拍戏教学法**<br>Tip 1：确定演员　Tip 2：确定出场顺序<br>**Para. 1:** Several minutes passed, but no help came.<br>承上　演员：I & Mrs. Lim<br>Mrs. Lim：情况变得更加糟糕<br>I: 我边安慰她，边不停地按警报<br>Tip 3：戏份不够，细节或环境来凑<br>I: 帮助 Mrs. Lim 放松<br>Mrs. Lim &I: 听到脚步声<br>启下<br>**Para. 2:** Bang! My hopes were lifted when I heard the firefighters on the other side of the lift door.<br>承上　演员：I & Mrs. Lim&the firefighters<br>one of the firefighters: 告诉我们别害怕<br>Mrs. Lim & I: 松了一口气<br>the firefighters：努力营救我们<br>Mrs. Lim &I: 获救了　故事结局<br>表示感谢 + 难忘的经历<br>情感态度价值观升华 | Part 1:<br>What were the main characters in Para.1 and 2?<br>Part 2:<br>1. What might happen to Mrs. Lim?<br>2. What might happen before we heard the firefighters?<br>3. How did we feel and react when we heard the firefighters?<br>4. What was the ending of the story?<br>5. What insights did I gain from this experience?<br>6. What did we do in such an emergency?<br>7. How did the firefighters help us out of the lift? | 利用五五拍戏教学法，引导学生搭建合理、有逻辑且连贯的续写情节 |

续表

<table>
<tr><th>阶段</th><th>活动形式及步骤</th><th>问题链</th><th>设计意图</th></tr>
<tr><td>语言表达</td><td>1. 结合搭建的续写框架，撰写草稿<br>语言表达：列草稿<br>Para. 1: Several minutes passed, but no help came.<br>承上　演员：I & Mrs. Lim<br>Mrs. Lim：情况变得更加糟糕<br>I: 我边安慰她，边不停地按警报<br>Tip 3：戏份不够，环境或细节来凑<br>I: 唱歌来帮助 Mrs. Lim 放松<br>Mrs. Lim &I: 听到脚步声<br>启下<br>• Mrs. Lim's condition was getting worse and worse.<br>• I comforted her as I continued pressing the emergency bell.<br>• There was still no response.<br>• I tried to sing to help her relax.<br>• We heard the footsteps approaching.<br>2. 借助点线面润色升级法润色草稿，并标记微场景<br>语言表达：升级表达（微场景＋公式技巧）<br>Para. 1: Several minutes passed, but no help came.<br>Mrs. Lim's condition was getting worse and worse.<br>【微场景：被困电梯中的细节描写】<br>点：精细化用词（tremble）<br>线：动作链<br>面：环境描写（with 结构）<br>With the air growing thin, Mrs. Lim was breathless and trembling with fear, her hands gripping mine tightly.<br>I comforted her as I continued pressing the emergency bell.<br>I patted her gently while I continued pressing the emergency bell, hoping that someone would notice us being trapped.<br>【微场景：努力求救】<br>点：精细化用词（pat）<br>线：动作链<br>面：心理描写（hoping...）</td><td>1. What would you do to polish your draft?<br>2. What techniques can be used to polish your writing?</td><td>1. 通过使用点线面润色升级法，帮助学生提高写作表达水平，使表达更加精准丰富<br>2. 梳理微场景设计和写作公式，引导学生将润色技巧迁移应用到类似话题的描写中</td></tr>
<tr><td>连句成篇</td><td>以“词→短语→句子”循序渐进的方式将通过以上环节润色的十句话连句成篇，完成初稿<br>连句成篇<br>请注意连接成分，并进行分类。<br>连接成分：副词 ②③⑤；短语 ①④⑦；句子 ⑥<br>Several minutes passed, but no help came. ① With the air growing thin, Mrs. Lim became breathless and trembled with fear, her hands gripping mine tightly. I patted her gently while I continued pressing the emergency bell, hoping that someone would notice us being trapped. ② Unfortunately, there was still no response. Hopeless as I was, I tried to help Mrs. Lim relax. “We will be fine!” a voice inside assured me. ③ Soon, we heard footsteps approaching.<br>Bang! My hopes were lifted when I heard the firefighters on the other side of the lift door. “Don't be afraid, we're here to help!” said one of the firefighters. ④ Hearing the comforting voice, we breathed in relief like a heavy stone removed from us. ⑤ Then I heard the sound of tools against the metal door. ⑥ As the door finally opened, the firefighters, wearing bright helmets and warm smiles, extended their hands to help us out. ⑦ After stepping out of the lift, we embraced, tears of joy and relief streaming down our faces. “Thank you!Without your timely rescue, we might die.” We repeatedly expressed our gratitude. What an eventful but unforgettable day!</td><td>What techniques can be employed to make the above sentences flow smoothly and coherently?</td><td>运用“词→短语→句子”的方法，使语言衔接更加有序</td></tr>
<tr><td>点评初稿</td><td>结合评价量表进行自评和互评【详见附录一和附录二】</td><td>Based on the evaluation criteria, what useful advice would you give to your peer?</td><td>根据评价量表，引导学生发现同伴写作的优势并改进自己存在的问题，提高写作水平</td></tr>
<tr><td>润色习作</td><td>根据评价反馈，润色修改课堂习作</td><td>1. How could you refine your writing based on the feedback?<br>2. What useful tips could you use to finish other writing tasks?</td><td>拓展话题内容，巩固课堂所学</td></tr>
</table>

## 附录 1：真题文本

① When we were finally dismissed from the last class of the day, the students streamed out of the classrooms. It was another boring day after school. I dragged my feet home as I sighed. Yet another uneventful day, I thought. Little did I know that the day would take a turn for the worse.

② The lift lobby（电梯间）of my flat was old and dirty. The walls, which were painted white, had been dirtied over many years. I reached my flat's lobby, and pressed the lift button and went in. Just then, Mrs. Lim, my elderly neighbor, hobbled（蹒跚）in. She looked ancient with tissue paper white hair, wearing a faded old-fashioned dress. I held the lift door open, flashing a friendly smile, and politely greeted her. I asked her how she felt that day and pressed the buttons. She thanked me for being so polite, then we were silent for the rest of the ride.

③ The lift fell down increasingly fast. There were loud clanking sounds here and there while the lift grew slower and slower. My heart beat hard and fast as my hands turned cold and wet with sweat. Unfortunately, the lift came to an abrupt stop at the fifth floor. I pressed the buttons hard several times, but it was of no help. The lights on the buttons had gone out. It soon dawned on me that we were trapped. An icy fear crept up my spine. Mrs. Lim was hysterical（歇斯底里的）.

④ "We will never get out!" she cried with her face pale. It had become a colorless mask. I had no time to lose. I pressed the bell in the lift immediately. The sound was surely deafening, but what other choice did I have? Mrs. Lim burst into tears. I tried my very best to comfort her, telling her that everything would be all right and that we needed to find out how to get out safely. Mrs. Lim began having trouble breathing, and I immediately helped her sit down and loosened her collar.

**注意**

1. 续写词数应为 150 个左右；
2. 请按如下格式在答题卡的相应位置作答。

Several minutes passed, but no help came. ____________________

____________________

Bang! My hopes were lifted when I heard the firefighters on the other side of the lift door. ____

____________________

## 附录 2: 参考范文

**Several minutes passed, but no help came.** With the air growing thin, Mrs. Lim became breathless and trembled with fear, her hands gripping mine tightly. I patted her gently while I continued pressing the emergency bell, hoping that someone would notice us being trapped. Unfortunately, there was still no response. Hopeless as I was, I tried to help Mrs. Lim relax. "We will be fine!" a voice inside assured me. Soon, we heard footsteps approaching.

**Bang! My hopes were lifted when I heard the firefighters on the other side of the lift door.** "Don't be afraid. We're here to help!" said one of the firefighters. Hearing the comforting voice, we breathed in relief like a heavy stone removed from us. Then I heard the sound of tools against the metal door. As the door finally opened, the firefighters, wearing bright helmets and warm smiles, extended their hands to help us out. After stepping out of the lift, we embraced, tears of joy and relief streaming down our faces. "Thank you! Without your timely rescue, we might die." We repeatedly expressed our gratitude. What an eventful but unforgettable day!

## 附录 3：2024 年大湾区二模续写试题

① After a busy week, Emily and her parents decided to go on a mountain picnic. They longed to fully experience nature's beauty and enjoy quality family time. Little did they know, this outing would be filled with unexpected twists and turns（波折）.

② Arriving at the mountain's base, they discovered a house, in front of which Mike and his father had just finished loading a boat onto Mike's truck. Emily approached them and asked for the best picnic spot in the area. Knowing the mountain well, Mike suggested a location about two hours' walk away. "It's worth the effort," he assured them.

③ Parking their car next to Mike's truck and carrying their picnic supplies, Emily and her parents set off on the winding road. Tall green trees on one side, a flowing stream on the other, the road eventually led them to a breathtaking clearing dotted with colorful wildflowers. They enjoyed their delicious sandwiches, fruits, and snacks, engaging in pleasant conversations.

④ Just as they finished their meal and settled down to relax, dark clouds unexpectedly rolled in. It looked like rain. Panicked, they hurriedly set up the tent they had brought. No sooner had they entered than raindrops began pouring on the roof. Heavy rain enveloped the surroundings, making it impossible to see anything. They had no choice but to patiently wait it out.

⑤ After what felt like a century, the rain ceased. Emily and her parents wasted no time packing up their belongings, ready to get downhill. However, their excitement turned to worry when they discovered that the small stream they had previously crossed had turned into a wide and impassable river. With no cellphone signal, they were trapped without a means of seeking help. To make matters worse, darkness was approaching.

注意

1. 续写词数应为 150 个左右；
2. 请按如下格式在答题卡的相应位置作答。

Suddenly, they heard the sound of a vehicle from across the river.__________

________________________________________

Emily and her parents boarded the boat.________________________________

________________________________________

# 第四节 以 2022 年新高考Ⅰ、Ⅱ卷真题为例的读后续写教学设计案例

## 一、文本分析

**What** 本文的主题语境为“人与社会”，涉及“个人成长”的内容。故事发生在一个小镇，主要讲述七所不同小学的学生参加一场越野长跑比赛。“我”作为一名特殊教育教师，在大赛当天，发现患有大脑病患的小学生 David 独自站在一旁。“我”询问其原因，他表示准备放弃比赛。因为教练担心同学们会嘲笑 David，所以想让 David 自己决定是否参加赛跑。

续写第一段的段首句：“我们”坐在一起，但是 David 不看“我”。

续写第二段的段首句：“我”看着 David 和其他选手一起朝着起跑线走去。

根据续写两段的首句内容，可以预测后面的故事情节：“我”和 David 沟通后，David 最终参赛，并坚持完成比赛。

**Why** 本文通过 David 的故事，强调了理解和尊重特殊学生的身体状况，突出了个体差异的重要性。故事传递了每个孩子都应有平等参与的机会。通过对 David 的关怀，教师不仅履行了职责，更给予了 David 人格成长的认同和鼓励。故事通过这种方式强调了包容性教育的重要性，即社会和教育者应当以平等和尊重的态度对待每个孩子，为他们提供表达和发展的平台。

**How** 故事采用了“冲突——解决”的结构，通过描写 David 内心的矛盾与挣扎，以及教师如何提供支持，推动了情节的发展。文章通过细腻的心理描写，深入刻画了 David 与教师内心的波动与情感变化，增强了故事的情感深度。特别是文章通过呈现 David 在学校的表现及他如何逐步完成挑战、为比赛做准备的具体细节，展现了 David

不断突破自我、追求进步的过程。通过这些生动的细节刻画，故事更加真实、感人，唤起读者的情感共鸣，使他们更深刻地理解教师与学生之间的关系，以及成长与挑战的主题。

## 二、学情分析

基本信息：高一学生，班级人数：60 人；平均分：90 分左右；读后续写平均分：13 分左右。

| 项目 | 内容 |
|---|---|
| 已有基础 | 1. 已经了解读后续写这一题型，并具有基本的读写技能<br>2. 能够梳理出 who、when、where 等浅层信息<br>3. 熟悉“成长类”话题 |
| 存在障碍 | 1. 不能梳理出故事的情节发展及主要人物的情感变化<br>2. 不能准确分析人物并提炼情感、态度和价值观<br>3. 续写框架比较混乱，情节不合理，偏离文章主题<br>4. 不会用多样化的语言来刻画人物从焦虑到自信的情感变化<br>5. 不了解评分标准 |
| 发展需求 | 1. 梳理语篇的情节发展和主要人物的情感变化，并学会从多角度进行刻画<br>2. 学会分析文本中关于 who、how、why 等的深层信息<br>3. 建构合理的续写框架<br>4. 提升语言表达技能，确保续写语言准确、生动，兼顾衔接和连贯<br>5. 熟悉续写评价要点 |
| 解决措施 | 1. 借助六何分析法开展语篇分析，精准把握故事核心要素<br>2. 借助故事山梳理故事情节和情感两条线，精准把握故事走向<br>3. 借助五五拍戏教学法，构建合理的续写情节和框架<br>4. 借助点线面润色升级法和连句成篇技巧，丰富语言表达，提高语篇连贯性<br>5. 借助精细化评价标准，开展有针对性的润色修改 |

## 三、教学目标

通过本节课，学生能够：

**语言能力**

1. 通过分析文中对 David 的描述，理解并运用描述复杂情感、身体状态的词汇和表达方式，如“rock from side to side” “swing his feet forward” 和“big toothy smile is absent”，提升语言表达的精准度和丰富性。

2. 描述面对挑战时，运用对话和细节描写表达人物情感，提升语言表达能力。

**文化意识**

1. 通过了解 David 的故事，理解并尊重个体差异，关注特殊儿童群体的情感与需求，激发接纳自我不足并勇于突破自我的意识。

2. 通过分析教练和教师的行为，理解成人在儿童教育中的作用，并思考成人如何帮助儿童建立自信并改善社会适应能力。

**思维品质**

1. 运用六何分析法多角度分析人物、情节和背景，理解人物选择背后的动机及其结果，培养批判性思维能力。

2. 运用五五拍戏教学法，合理预测续写的情节发展，培养逻辑思维与问题解决能力。

**学习能力**

1. 通过互评与自评的方式，提升自我修正和反思能力，进一步提高写作水平。

2. 运用所学的分析方法，构建并修改自己的写作框架，提升自主学习和创新能力。

## 四、教学思路

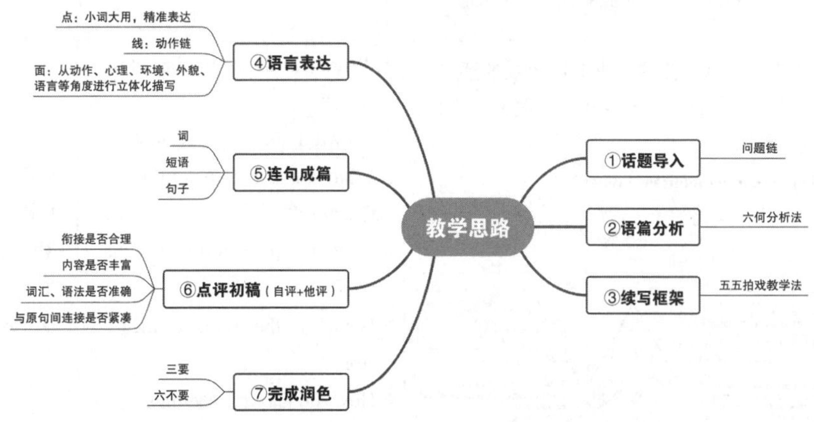

## 五、教学过程

| 阶段 | 活动形式及步骤 | 问题链 | 设计意图 |
| --- | --- | --- | --- |
| 话题导入 | 1. 问题探讨：你是否曾经遇到过感觉自己与别人不同的时刻？这种差异让你遇到哪些困难或者挑战，你是如何克服的？<br>2. 小组活动：分享你或你身边的人在面对类似挑战时的故事或经历。<br>情境创设：想象你是图中的小男孩，面对一项自己感到很难完成的任务，比如一个比赛或者挑战。如果你是他，你会有什么样的情绪？你会怎么做？ | 1. Have you ever encountered a situation where you felt different from others?<br>2. What challenges did it bring, and how did you overcome them?<br>3. Who would like to share a personal experience or a story of someone you know who faced similar challenges?<br>4. Imagine you are in his place, facing a challenge or task that feels very difficult. How would you feel? What would you do? | 激发学生对“面对挑战”和“自我突破”的兴趣，引导他们从个人经历中提取情感共鸣，并通过换位思考帮助学生更好地理解故事情境和人物心理。 |
| 语篇分析 | 1. 快速浏览文章，按照六何分析法提取文本的浅层信息（when/where/who）<br>**语篇分析**<br>① It was the day of the big cross-country run. Students from seven different primary schools in and around the small town were warming up and walking the route（路线）through thick evergreen forest.<br>② I looked around and finally spotted David, who was standing by himself off to the side by a fence...<br>④ I quickly searched the crowd for the school's coach and asked him what had happened.<br>**六何分析法**<br>when: the day of the big cross-country run; what: Story mountain<br>where: the route through a thick evergreen forest near a small town; how: analyze narrative perspective and style<br>who: David, I, the coach, the crowd; why: analyze the purpose | 1.When did the story take place?<br>2.Where did the story take place?<br>3.Who were the main characters in the text? | 运用六何分析法，梳理文本的基本要素 |
| | 2. 借助故事山结构梳理文本的情节及情感、态度变化（what），包括开端、发展、冲突、解决和结局<br>**情节分析——story mountain【what】**<br>Para. 5:<br>• Despite his strict preparation, David hesitated and decided not to run.<br>• David: fearful, conflicted<br>Para. 2–4:<br>• I approached David to inquire about his unusual behavior and learned the coach's concerns about potential challenges.<br>• David: hesitant, vulnerable<br>续写：<br>• Influenced by the reassuranced from his teacher, David might reconsider his decision.<br>• David: willing, confident?<br>Para. 1:<br>• Students from seven different primary schools were warming up for the race and David stood aside without a smile.<br>• David: isolated, uneasy<br>续写：<br>• What happened to David?<br>• David: (potentially) determined, hopeful? | 1. What was the beginning of the story?<br>2.How did the story develop?<br>3.What was the main conflict of the story?<br>4.What was the resolution of the conflict?<br>5.What was the ending of the story?<br>6.How did David's feelings change? | 运用故事山梳理文本的情节和情感两条线，引导学生关注故事走向和情感变化 |

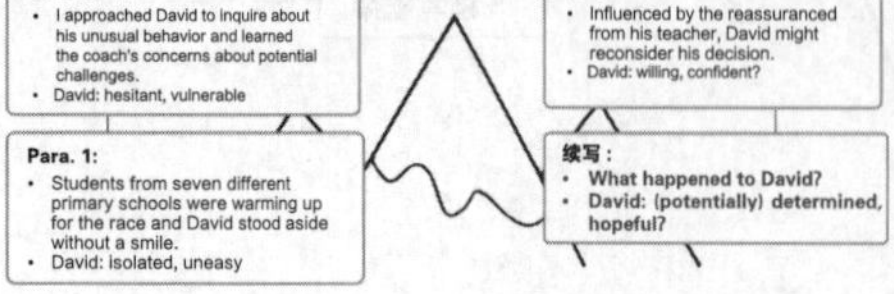

续表

| 阶段 | 活动形式及步骤 | 问题链 | 设计意图 |
| --- | --- | --- | --- |
| 语篇分析 | 3. 标记出文本中有关主人公的描写和介绍，进行人物分析 (who)<br>**人物分析【who】**<br>David<br>• His usual big toothy smile was absent today.<br>• David had not missed a single practice, and although he always finished his run long after the other children, he did always finish.<br>• He had worked so hard!<br>**David was optimistic, determined, courageous, resilient and inspirational.**<br>I (the teacher)<br>• I quickly searched the crowd for the school's coach and asked him what had happened.<br>• As a special education teacher, I was familiar with the challenges David faced and was proud of his strong determination.<br>**I was empathetic, caring and protective.** | 1. Which sentences can show the characters' personalities?<br>2. What are the characters' personalities? | 关注故事主要人物的描写和分析，确保续写内容走向不偏离人物特征 |
| | 4. 分析文本的叙述视角和语言风格 (how)<br>**叙述视角与语言风格分析【how】**<br>Narrative perspective<br>• I looked around and finally spotted David, who was standing by himself off to the side by a fence.<br>**第一人称视角：I**<br>Narrative style<br>• I bit back my frustration.<br>• I was familiar with the challenges David faced and was proud of his strong determination.<br>• David had a brain disease which prevented him from walking or running like other children...<br>• His usual big toothy smile was absent today.<br>**语言风格：specific, direct, brief** | 1. What is the narrative perspective of this article?<br>2. What is the narrative style of this article? | 关注文本的叙述视角和语言风格，确保续写内容语言与原文的协同性 |
| | 5. 提炼分析文本的情感、态度和价值观 (why)<br>**情感、态度、价值观分析【why】**<br>人与自我<br>Perseverance and Courage<br>Autonomy and Self-Determination<br>人与社会<br>Inclusiveness and Equality | 1. Why do you think David decided not to participate in the race? What attitude might he have? Were there other choices for him?<br>2. What values or life perspectives does the story convey? | 引导学生深入思考故事中蕴含的情感、态度及价值观，进一步理解作者的意图 |
| 续写框架 | 使用五五拍戏教学法构建一个续写框架（每个段落都续写五个句子，两段续写句子的编号为1—10），并结合情节续写，从承上启下、故事结局和情感、态度和价值观等角度，提供拍戏建议<br>Tip 1：确定演员<br>Tip 2：确定出场顺序<br>Tip 3：戏份不够，细节或环境来凑 | Part 1:<br>What were the main characters in Para.1 and 2?<br>Part 2:<br>1. When David wouldn't look at me, what might happen to him next?<br>2. Before I watched David moving up to the starting line, what might happen?<br>3. How would you describe the atmosphere and setting when David was at the starting line? | 提供清晰的续写框架（五五拍戏教学法），引导学生构建合理的故事情节 |

续表

| 阶段 | 活动形式及步骤 | 问题链 | 设计意图 |
|---|---|---|---|
| 续写框架 | **续写框架：五五拍戏教学法**<br>Tip 1：确定演员<br>Tip 2：确定出场顺序<br>**Para. 1:** We sat down next to each other, but David wouldn't look at me.<br>承上<br>演员：David & I<br>① David: 脸色显得有些苍白，双手紧紧握着<br>⑥ I: 注意到他脚尖不断地点地<br>⑦ I: 轻轻地触碰他的肩膀，试图用行动传达支持<br>Tip 3：戏份不够，细节或环境来凑<br>② David: 向起跑线走去<br>启下<br>**Para. 2:** I watched as David moved up to the starting line with the other runners.<br>承上<br>演员：David & I/coach/other runners<br>③ David: 逐渐加快了步伐<br>⑧ David: 变得坚定<br>⑨ the crowd: 为 David 加油<br>故事结局<br>④ David: 和其他孩子一起冲出起跑线<br>⑤ David 的勇敢激励了在场的每一个人<br>情感态度价值观升华 | 4. In the end, how did David overcome the challenges?<br>5. What values or life lessons does the story convey?<br>6. What would I do to help David?<br>7. With my encouragement, what would David behave?<br>8. How would you describe the atmosphere in part 1?<br>9. What challenges or conflicts could arise during the race, considering David's condition?<br>10. What might David do to overcome the conflicts or challenges? | |
| 语言表达 | 1. 结合续写框架，撰写草稿<br>**语言表达：列草稿**<br>**Para. 1:** We sat down next to each other, but David wouldn't look at me.<br>承上<br>演员：David & I<br>① David: 脸色显得有些苍白，双手紧紧握着<br>⑥ I：注意到他脚尖不断地点地<br>⑦ I: 轻轻地触碰他的肩膀，试图用行动传达支持<br>Tip 3：戏份不够，细节或环境来凑<br>② David: 向起跑线走去<br>启下<br>• His face was pale, and his hands were tightly clasped.<br>• I noticed his toes tapping on the ground.<br>• I gently touched his shoulder, trying to offer some support.<br>• The preparatory whistle blew.<br>• He walked towards the starting line.<br>2. 教师示范讲解如何运用点线面润色升级法润色草稿，并标记微场景<br>**语言表达微技能：点线面润色升级法**<br>点：具体的某个动作<br>线：将动作进行拆解形成一条动作链<br>面：多面立体化 外貌描写 环境描写 语言描写 心理描写<br>3. 润色草稿，并梳理升级思路（说明：为了突出思路，这里将每个句子都做了升级。考试时不需要将每个句子都升级。）<br>**语言表达：升级表达**<br>I gently touched his shoulder, trying to offer some support.<br>【微场景：表示安慰】<br>面：动作描写+语言描写（直接引语）<br>I gently touched his shoulder, trying to offer some support, and whispered, "You don't have to do this if you're not ready."<br>He walked towards the starting line.<br>【微场景：走向起跑线】<br>线：动作链（+状语）<br>面：动作描写+外貌描写（独立主格结构）<br>After a moment of silence, he took a deep breath, slowly stood up, and walked determinedly towards the starting line, his eyes filled with confidence. | 1. How would you do to polish your draft?<br>2. What techniques can be used to polish your writing? | 通过点线面润色升级法，帮助学生提高写作表达水平，使表达更加精准、丰富 |

续表

| 阶段 | 活动形式及步骤 | 问题链 | 设计意图 |
| --- | --- | --- | --- |
| 连句成篇 | 以“词→短语→句子”循序渐进的方式将润色的十句话连句成篇，完成初稿<br>**连句成篇**<br>连接成分：副词 ③；短语 ①②④⑧；句子 ⑤⑥⑦<br>***Paragraph 1: We sat down next to each other, but David wouldn't look at me.*** His face was pale, and his hands were tightly clasped.① Apart from these, I noticed his toes tapping on the ground, a habit he has when he's anxious, which made me more concerned about him. ②Sensing his discomfort, I gently touched his shoulder and whispered, "You don't have to do this if you're not ready." ③Soon,the preparatory whistle blew. ④Much to my surprise, he took a deep breath, slowly stood up, and walked towards the starting line, his eyes filled with newfound confidence.<br>***Paragraph 2: I watched as David moved up to the starting line with the other runners.*** He shook his head as if to chase away the fears inside him and then began to quicken his pace. ⑤As he approached the starting line, his steps became more determined, and⑥after hearing the cheers from the crowd, his confidence seemed to grow even stronger.⑦The minute the starting gun sounded, David and the other children burst from the starting line.⑧At that very moment, not only did David show everyone his courage to overcome physical limitations, but he also inspired everyone present. | What techniques can be employed to make the above sentences flow smoothly and coherently? | 运用“词→短语→句子”的方法，使语言衔接更加有序 |
| 点评初稿 | 结合评价量表进行自评和互评【详见附录一和附录二】 | Based on the evaluation criteria, what useful advice would you give to your peers? | 提供详细的评分标准，使学生在写作时更具针对性，明确评价要点 |
| 润色习作 | 结合评价反馈润色自己的习作 | How could you refine your writing based on the feedback? | 结合同伴反馈，润色并完善写作内容 |

## 附录 1：真题文本

①It was the day of the big cross-country run. Students from seven different primary schools in and around the small town were warming up and walking the route（路线）through thick evergreen forest.

②I looked around and finally spotted David, who was standing by himself off to the side by a fence. He was small for ten years old. His usual big toothy smile was absent today. I walked over and asked him why he wasn't with the other children. He hesitated and then said he had decided not to run.

③What was wrong? He had worked so hard for this event!

④I quickly searched the crowd for the school's coach and asked him what had happened. “I was afraid that kids from other schools would laugh at him,” he explained uncomfortably. “I gave him the choice to run or not, and let him decide.”

⑤ I bit back my frustration（懊恼）. I knew the coach meant well—he thought he was doing the right thing. After making sure that David could run if he wanted, I turned to find him coming towards me, his small body rocking from side to side as he swung his feet forward.

⑥ David had a brain disease which prevented him from walking or running like other children, but at school his classmates thought of him as a regular kid. He always participated to the best of his ability in whatever they were doing. That was why none of the children thought it unusual that David had decided to join the cross-country team. It just took him longer—that's all. David had not missed a single practice, and although he always finished his run long after the other children, he did always finish. As a special education teacher at the school, I was familiar with the challenges David faced and was proud of his strong determination.

**注意**

1. 续写词数应为 150 个左右；
2. 请按如下格式在答题卡的相应位置作答。

We sat down next to each other, but David wouldn't look at me. ____________________

______________________________________________________________________

I watched as David moved up to the starting line with the other runners. ______________

______________________________________________________________________

附录 2：参考范文

**We sat down next to each other, but David wouldn't look at me.** His face was pale, and his hands were tightly clasped. Apart from these, I noticed his toes tapping on the ground, a habit he has when he's anxious, which made me more concerned about him. Sensing his discomfort, I gently touched his shoulder and whispered, "You don't have to do this if you're not ready." Soon, the preparatory whistle blew. Much to my surprise, he took a deep breath, slowly stood up, and walked towards the starting line, his eyes filled with newfound confidence.

**I watched as David moved up to the starting line with the other runners.** He shook his head as if to chase away the fears inside him and then began to quicken his pace. As he approached the starting line, his steps became more determined, and after hearing the cheers from the crowd, his confidence seemed to grow even stronger. The minute the starting gun sounded, David and the other children burst from the starting line. At that very moment, not only did David show everyone his courage to overcome physical limitations, but he also inspired everyone present.

# 第五节

## 以 2024 届广东高三六校第三次联考试题卷为例的读后续写教学设计案例

### 一、文本分析

**What** 本文主题语境是“人与自我”，涉及“优秀品行、正确的生活态度、公民的义务与社会责任”等内容。本文讲述了“我”和五岁的儿子 Henry 在消防局开放日观看消防车模型的经历。Henry 对消防车和消防员的工作产生了浓厚的兴趣，并询问他们何时能玩这些消防车模型。新年将至，“我”想借此机会让 Henry 理解新年的意义不仅是收礼物，还应该包括关心那些在节日期间无法与家人团聚的人们。受参观消防局的启发，Henry 提出想在新年跟消防员一起玩玩具，但却被告知消防员都很忙。

续写第一段的段首句：“或者我们可以给他们买点别的东西。”Henry 自言自语。

续写第二段的段首句：我把这些照片发布到了网上。

根据续写两段的段首句内容，可以预测后面的故事情节：Henry 为消防员准备了礼物，让他们在工作的时候也能感到温暖和关怀。“我”记录了赠送礼物的整个过程，并将照片发布到网上，这些照片受到了网友们的关注，激励了更多人关心和支持身边的无名英雄。

**Why** 本文通过描述“我”和儿子的日常生活经历，传递了帮助他人、尊重他人职业和感恩的价值观。“我”教育 Henry 关爱他人，并鼓励他思考如何帮助他人，让 Henry 成为一个有爱心、有责任感的人。同时，本文也向读者展示了消防员工作的重要性和辛苦。

**How** 本文以第一人称的视角讲述“我”和儿子 Henry 的日常生活经历，展示了亲子教育的过程和主题。文章语言简洁明了，以对话和叙述相结合的方式生动地展现了事件的整个过程。对话的形式增加了故事的可读性和真实感。

## 二、学情分析

**基本信息：高一学生，班级人数：60人；平均分：70分左右；续写平均分：10分左右。**

| 项目 | 内容 |
|---|---|
| 已有基础 | 1. 已经了解读后续写这一题型<br>2. 能够梳理出 who、when、where 等浅层信息<br>3. 能够根据提示句构建续写内容的基本方向 |
| 存在障碍 | 1. 不能梳理出故事的明线（情节线）和暗线（情感线）<br>2. 不能准确分析人物和提炼情感、态度和价值观<br>3. 续写内容比较混乱，缺乏逻辑，甚至偏离文章主题<br>4. 语言表达中出现大量词汇及语法错误 |
| 发展需求 | 1. 梳理故事情节发展和主要人物的情感变化<br>2. 建构合理的续写框架<br>3. 提升语言表达技能，确保续写语言准确生动，兼顾衔接和过渡 |
| 解决措施 | 1. 借助六何分析法开展语篇分析，精准把握故事核心要素<br>2. 借助故事山梳理故事情节和情感两条线，精准把握故事走向<br>3. 借助五五拍戏教学法，构建合理的续写情节和框架<br>4. 借助点线面润色升级法和连句成篇技巧，提升语言表达 |

## 三、教学目标

通过本节课，学生能够：

**语言能力**

1. 理解并运用表达人物情感和行为的词汇和句式，准确描述人物的内心世界与反应。

2. 使用因果关系和条件句等句式，提升语言的连贯性和逻辑性。

3. 赏析并模仿故事中人物的语言风格，根据不同情境灵活调整表达方式。

3. 通过识别和模仿故事中人物语言的多样性，如孩子的直接询问和成人的解释性回答，学生可以学会根据不同的听众调整语言风格。

**文化意识**

1. 理解并讨论新年等节日的深层文化意义。

2. 增强对消防员等公共安全职业的尊重和理解，了解这些从业人员对社会的贡献。

3. 培养参加社区服务和帮助他人的意识。

**思维品质**

1. 学会运用六何分析法从情节、人物行为和心理等角度分析文本，理解文本的深层含义和叙事的意图提升逻辑推理能力。

2. 学会运用五五拍戏教学法合理设置故事情节确保续写内容的合理性和连贯性。

**学习能力**

提取文本关键信息，并通过自主探索和小组协作，设计合理的续写情节，同时提升信息处理能力、主动学习意识和团队合作能力。

## 四、教学思路

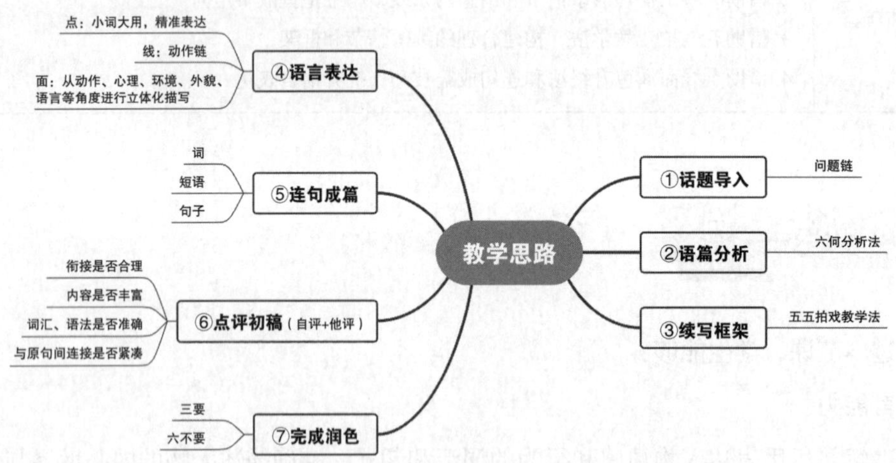

## 五、教学过程

<table>
<tr><th>阶段</th><th>活动形式及步骤</th><th>问题链</th><th>设计意图</th></tr>
<tr><td>话题导入</td><td>观察消防员工作日常的图片，思考并回答相关问题 </td><td>1. What are the duties of the firefighters?<br>2. What gifts would you want to give them if you had a chance to visit the firefighters on New Year's Day?</td><td>借助图片，激发学生的阅读兴趣和已有认知，为后续阅读做铺垫</td></tr>
<tr><td rowspan="3">语篇分析</td><td>1. 快速浏览文本，按照六何分析法提取文本的三要素（when/where/who）<br>语篇分析<br>① It was October and we were attending the fire hall's open house with our five-year-old son Henry. He was especially drawn to the collection of model fire trucks in the large glass display case. The firefighters were more than happy to answer his many questions about each piece of equipment. "When do you get to play with those?" Henry asked the accompanying firefighter.<br>④ With colder weather setting in, our thoughts turned to the upcoming New Year's Day.<br>六何分析法<br>when: in October and the upcoming New Year's Day<br>where: at a fire hall during an open house and later at the family's home<br>who: Henry, a five-year-old boy, his parents and firefighters<br>what: Story mountain<br>how: analyze the narrative perspective and style<br>why: analyze the purpose</td><td>1. When did the story take place?<br>2. Where did the story take place?<br>3. Who were the main characters in the text?</td><td>按照六何分析法提取文本基本要素</td></tr>
<tr><td>2. 运用故事山梳理文本的情节和情感线（what）<br>情节分析——story mountain【what】<br>Para. 1:<br>• We attended an open house at a fire hall in October. Henry was drawn to a collection of model fire trucks displayed in a glass case.<br>• Henry: curious and excited<br>Para. 2–3:<br>• A firefighter explained that the model fire trucks were not toys to play with, which made Henry lose in thought as they walked home.<br>• Henry: disappointed and confused<br>Para. 4–6:<br>• We wanted to educate Henry about the true spirit of New Year celebration. Henry wanted to take presents to the firefighers.<br>• Henry: considerate and empathetic<br>Para. 7–8:<br>• Henry's father gently corrected his misunderstanding by explaining the serious responsibilities of the firefighters.<br>• Henry: serious<br>续写：<br>• What happened to Henry and his family?<br>• Henry: (potentially) creative and favorable?</td><td>1. What was the beginning of the story?<br>2. How did the story develop?<br>3. What was the main conflict of the story?<br>4. What was the resolution of the conflict?<br>5. What was the ending of the story?<br>6. How did Henry's feelings change?</td><td>运用故事山梳理文本的情节、情感两条线，引导学生关注故事走向和情感变化</td></tr>
<tr><td>3. 标记出文本中有关主人公的描写和介绍，进行人物分析 (who)<br>人物分析【who】<br>Parents<br>• The last thing we wanted was our kid seeing the festival as merely a time to receive love and gifts.<br>• We explained that every one of us can be of some help to those in need.<br>• Well, that is a good idea, but they don't really have time to play with toys because they are too busy keeping us safe during the holiday, just like those policemen and doctors.<br>Parents were educative, supportive, and patient.<br>Henry<br>• He was especially drawn to the collection of model fire trucks in the large glass display case.<br>• When do you get to play with those?<br>• Can we take presents to the firefighters? They aren't allowed to play with all those fire trucks!<br>• Henry became very serious. He knew his dad was right.<br>Henry was curious, empathetic and innocent.</td><td>1. Which sentences can show the characters' personalities?<br>2. What are the characters' personalities?</td><td>关注文本中针对主要人物的描写并对其进行分析，确保续写内容走向不偏离人物特征</td></tr>
</table>

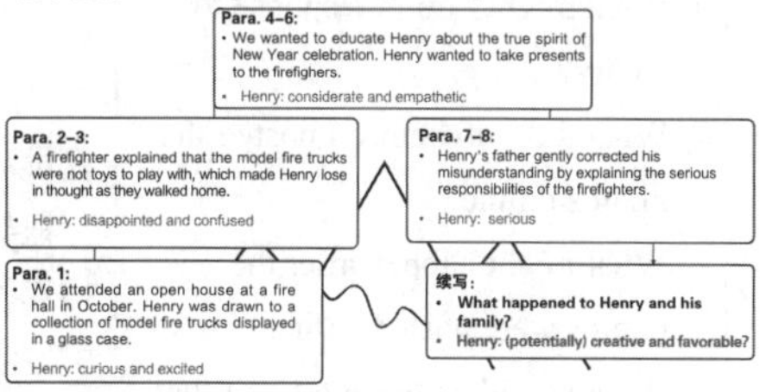

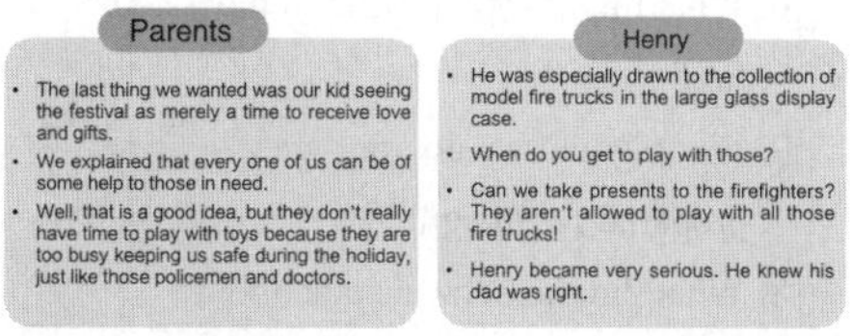

续表

| 阶段 | 活动形式及步骤 | 问题链 | 设计意图 |
|---|---|---|---|
| 语篇分析 | 4. 分析文本的叙述视角和语言风格 (how)<br>**叙述视角与语言风格【how】**<br>Narrative perspective<br>• We were attending the fire hall's open house with our five-year-old son Henry.<br>• We sat Henry down and explained that there were many children that didn't have toys to play with.<br>• I posted those photos online.<br>第一人称视角：We/I(the mother)<br>Narrative style<br>• He was especially drawn to the collection of model fire trucks in the large glass display case.<br>• When do you get to play with those?<br>• Henry's eyes shone! Can we take presents to the firefighters?<br>语言风格：descriptive; conversational; simple; clear | 1. What's the narrative perspective of the text?<br>2. What's the narrative style of the text? | 关注文本的叙述视角和语言风格，保障续写内容的语言与原文语言的协同性 |
| | 5. 分析文本的情感、态度和价值观（why）<br>**情感、态度、价值观分析【why】**<br>人与自我<br>Good conduct, citizen obligations and social responsibilities | What values or life perspectives does the story convey? | 引导学生深入思考文本中蕴含的情感、态度及价值观，进一步理解作者的意图 |
| 续写框架 | 使用五五拍戏教学法构建一个续写框架（每个段落都续写五个句子，两段续写句子的编号为 1—10），并结合情节进行续写，从承上启下、故事结局和情感、态度和价值观等角度，提供拍戏建议<br>Tip 1：确定演员<br>Tip 2：确定出场顺序<br>Tip 3：戏份不够，细节或环境来凑<br>**续写框架：五五拍戏教学法**<br>Tip 1：确定演员　Tip 2：确定出场顺序<br>Para. 1: "Or maybe we can bring them something else..." Henry murmured to himself.<br>承上　演员：Henry, I & firefighters<br>I: 思考要送什么特别的礼物<br>Henry: 提出送一个带有消防汽车玩具装饰的手工蛋糕<br>Henry and I：前往消防站送上礼物<br>Tip 3：戏份不够，细节或环境来凑<br>the firefighters: 很喜欢这个礼物，我拍下了这些感人的画面<br>启下<br>Para. 2: I posted those photos online.<br>承上　演员：we & other netizens<br>照片得到超级多点赞，并引发热议<br>other netizens: 提议发起一个特别的新年活动<br>we：发出倡议<br>故事结局<br>other netizens: 越来越多的人送出自己的礼物<br>Henry 明白了节日就是分享爱和礼物的时刻<br>情感、态度、价值观升华 | Part 1: What were the main characters in Para. 1 and Para. 2?<br>Part 2:<br>1. What might I do in response to Henry?<br>2. What did I do before I posted the photos online?<br>3. What might happen after the photos were posted online?<br>4. What would be the ending of the story?<br>5. What values or life lessons does the story convey?<br>6. What might Henry bring to the firefighters?<br>7. What would we do after we prepared for the gift?<br>8. What did the netizens talk about?<br>9. What was the event about? | 提供清晰的续写框架（五五拍戏教学法），引导学生构建合理的故事情节 |

续表

| 阶段 | 活动形式及步骤 | 问题链 | 设计意图 |
|---|---|---|---|
| 语言表达 | 1. 结合续写框架，撰写十句草稿<br>**语言表达：列草稿**<br>**Para. 2:** I posted those photos online.<br>照片得到超级多点赞，并引发热议 • The photos received a large number of likes and people began to talk about them.<br>提议发起一个特别的新年活动 • People launched a special New Year's event.<br>we：发出倡议 • We called on others to join.<br>other netizens: 越来越多的人送出自己的礼物 • More and more people sent out their own gifts.<br>Henry 明白了节日就是分享爱和礼物的时刻 • Henry came to understand that the festival is a time for sharing love and gifts.<br>2. 借助点线面润色升级法润色草稿，并标记微场景<br>**语言表达：升级表达（微场景+公式技巧）**<br>We called on others to join.<br>【微场景：呼吁参与】<br>点：精细化用词<br>面：情绪描写（形容词）<br>句式升级：举例子<br>Inspired, we appealed others to extend warmth to community helpers like doctors, nurses, and police officers.<br>More and more people sent out their own gifts.<br>【微场景：参与活动】<br>点：精细化用词<br>面：时间描写（介词短语）<br>Throughout the New Year period, an increasing number of people sent out their well-prepared gifts.<br>Henry came to understand that the festival is a time for sharing love and gifts.<br>【微场景：活动收获】<br>面：心理描写<br>句式升级：not just...but<br>Henry came to realize that the festival is not just a time for sharing love and gifts but a moment for spreading warmth. | 1. How would you polish your draft?<br>2. What techniques can be used to polish your writing? | 通过使用点线面润色升级法，帮助学生提高写作水平，使表达更加精准、丰富 |
| 连句成篇 | 以“词→短语→句子”循序渐进的方式将通过以上环节润色的十句话连句成篇，从而完成初稿<br>**连句成篇**<br>**请注意连接成分，并进行分类。**<br>连接成分：词 ②⑤；短语 ③④⑥⑦；句子 ①<br>***Paragraph 1:*** *“Or maybe we can bring them something else...” Henry murmured to himself.* ① As we gathered by the cozy fireplace, we considered the perfect gifts to give. ② Suddenly, Henry had an idea: why not bake a cake decorated with a model fire truck, accompanied by handmade New Year greeting cards? ③ Filled with excitement, we headed to deliver it just before New Year's Day. The firefighters raised the unique gift, exclaiming “We love this!” and I photographed these heartfelt moments that preserved the joy of our small gesture.<br>***Paragraph 2:*** *I posted those photos online.* They received millions of likes and sparked heated discussions. ④ Much to our surprise, one proposal for a special New Year's event ⑤ surprisingly earned the most thumbs-up! ⑥ Inspired by this, we appealed to our neighbours to extend their warmth to community helpers like doctors, nurses, and police officers. ⑦ Throughout the New Year period, more and more people began sending out their well-prepared gifts. Through this experience, Henry came to realize that the festival isn't merely about receiving gifts; it is a time for spreading warmth and kindness. | What techniques can be employed to make the above sentences flow smoothly and coherently? | 运用“词→短语→句子”的方法，使语言衔接更加有序 |
| 点评初稿 | 结合评价量表进行自评和互评【详见附录一和附录二】 | Based on the evaluation criteria, what useful advice would you give to your peers? | 提供详细的评分标准，使学生在创作时更具针对性，牢记评价要点 |
| 润色习作 | 结合评价反馈润色自己的习作 | How can you refine your writing based on the feedback? | 结合同伴反馈，润色并完善写作内容 |

## 附录 1：真题文本

① It was October and we were attending the fire hall's open house with our five-year-old son Henry. He was especially drawn to the collection of model fire trucks in the large glass display case. The firefighters were more than happy to answer his many questions about each piece of equipment. "When do you get to play with those?" Henry asked the accompanying firefighter.

② The firefighter hid his amusement and pretended to be serious as he answered. "We don't get to play with them. The chief keeps them locked away in that box."

③ Henry was lost in thought as we walked home that evening.

④ With colder weather setting in, our thoughts turned to the upcoming New Year's Day. It was important to us to educate Henry about the true spirit of New Year celebration. The last thing we wanted was our kid seeing the festival as merely a time to receive love and gifts.

⑤ We sat Henry down and explained that there were many children that didn't have toys to play with. Some children didn't have their mommy or dad for company during the festival because their parents were busy doing their jobs when we were on holiday. We explained that every one of us can be of some help to those in need.

⑥ Henry's eyes shone! "Can we take presents to the firefighters? They aren't allowed to play with all those fire trucks! We can take them toys to play with on New Year's Day!"

⑦ At first we didn't know how to respond. We had long since forgotten about the model fire trucks at the fire hall! Apparently Henry had not. His dad cleared his throat. "Well, that is a good idea, but they don't really have time to play with toys because they are too busy keeping us safe during the holiday, just like those policemen and doctors."

⑧ Henry became very serious. He knew his dad was right. Being a firefighter was a very important job.

**注 意**

1. 续写词数应为 150 个左右；

2. 请按如下格式在答题卡的相应位置作答。

"Or maybe we can bring them something else..." Henry murmured to himself. ___________

________________________________________________

I posted those photos online.____________________________________

________________________________________________

## 附录2：参考范文

**"Or maybe we can bring them something else..." Henry murmured to himself.** As we gathered by the cozy fireplace, we considered the perfect gifts to give. Suddenly, Henry had an idea: why not bake a cake decorated with a model fire truck, accompanied by handmade New Year greeting cards? Filled with excitement, we headed to deliver it just before New Year's Day. The firefighters raised the unique gift, exclaiming "We love this!" and I photographed these heartfelt moments that preserved the joy of our small gesture.

**I posted those photos online.** They received millions of likes and sparked heated discussions. Much to our surprise, one proposal for a special New Year's event surprisingly earned the most thumbs-up! Inspired by this, we appealed to our neighbors to extend their warmth to community helpers like doctors, nurses, and police officers. Throughout the New Year period, more and more people began sending out their well-prepared gifts. Through this experience, Henry came to realize that the festival isn't merely about receiving gifts; it is a time for spreading warmth and kindness.

# 第六节

# 以 2022 年 1 月浙江卷为例的读后续写教学设计案例

## 一、文本分析

**What** 本文的主题语境为“人与社会”，涉及“良好的人际关系与社会交往”等内容。故事讲述了“我”在心理学课上意外被安排与一位性格严肃、竞争力强的同学组队并合作完成项目的经历。虽然“我”一开始对此感到不安和担忧，但经过长时间的讨论，两人最终就青少年心理健康的研究主题达成了一致。

续写第一段的段首句：“我们”开始定期见面，共同制订我们的计划。

续写第二段的段首句：有一天“我”得知他因患重病住院了。

根据续写两段的首句内容，可以预测后面的故事情节：“我们”分工合作、讨论实验细节，并在合作的过程中慢慢消除了误会，关系也有所缓和。接着，“我”得知他因病住院，不得不独自完成任务。最后，通过前期的合作和后期“我”的努力，任务圆满完成了。“我”在这个过程中赢得了队友的尊重，并与其成了好友。

**Why** 本文描述“我”在面对不喜欢的队友时的内心挣扎和行动变化，传达了在困境中积极应对问题、勇于面对挑战的精神。尽管“我”最初对合作持有抵触和不安的情绪，但最终决定坚持下来，并与队友逐渐建立合作关系，这不仅展示了“我”的责任感和团队精神，也展现了在困难中个人成长的意义。

**How** 本文以第一人称视角生动地描述了“我”在心理学课程中被分配与一位性格严肃、竞争力强的同学合作的经历。语篇蕴含明暗两条线索：明线按照时间顺序展开，描述了“我”和队友通过分组、认识、讨论、确定题目，完成了这次项目的合作；暗线描述“我”从抗拒到逐渐接受队友的情感变化，细腻地刻画了“我”在合作过程中内心的挣扎与成长。

本文通过生动的描述性语言、大量细腻的心理描写增强了叙述的生动性和情绪的感染力。如第一段的“I secretly hoped... Above all, I hoped...”、第二段的“I felt he treated me as though I would hold him back”等心理描写，使读者能够深刻感受到“我”的不安与抗拒。同时，文章语言表达地道，灵活使用多种习语（如“as fate would have it”“take a nosedive”“being brushed off”“stopped short”“my chickening out”等）不仅增加了语篇的自然感和趣味性，也在一定程度上增加了文本理解的难度。

## 二、学情分析

**基本信息：高二学生，班级人数：54 人；平均分：95 分左右；读后续写平均分：12 分左右。**

| 项目 | 内容 |
| --- | --- |
| 已有基础 | 1. 能够较好地理解故事情节，分析人物性格<br>2. 能够运用基本的英语语法，构建简单的句子和段落 |
| 存在障碍 | 1. 不能准确梳理故事的情感线和分析人物性格，难以捕捉文章主旨<br>2. 难以在有限的时间内深入理解和构思续写内容<br>3. 续写内容存在语法错误和词汇误用的问题，使续写内容与原文风格不符<br>4. 续写内容句式单一，缺乏文采，难以生动描述同学之间的互动<br>5. 续写内容逻辑不清晰，并与原文脱节 |
| 发展需求 | 1. 学会梳理故事的情感线、情节线和分析人物性格，并总结文章的情感、态度和价值观<br>2. 提高情节搭建的质量和效率，确保续写内容结构清晰、层次分明<br>3. 提高语言表达的准确性，保证续写内容在语言风格和语篇衔接上与原文相协同<br>4. 使用丰富的句式描述同学之间的互动和情绪变化，增强文章的感染力 |
| 解决措施 | 1. 借助六何分析法和故事山，梳理文本，总结文章的情感、态度和价值观<br>2. 利用五五拍戏教学法，提高情节搭建的效率和质量<br>3. 利用点线面润色升级法，提高语言表达的准确性和丰富性 |

## 三、教学目标

通过本节课，学生能够：

**语言能力**

1. 通过赏析文本中关于人物心理活动的描写，学会使用以下短语和句子进行心理描写：

I secretly hoped… He just gave me the impression… I was uneasy… I actually wanted to drop the class at one point, but stopped short because I didn't want to give him the satisfaction of my chickening out.

2. 掌握点线面润色升级法，提升语言表达的准确性和丰富性。

**文化意识**

1. 通过分析人物合作的经历，理解积极沟通与协调在实现共同目标中的作用，培养合作意识。

2. 通过分析人物态度变化，认识到理解和适应不同文化间的差异是跨文化合作成功的关键。

**思维品质**

1. 学会运用六何分析法，梳理人物关系、情节发展和叙述手法，提升逻辑分析能力，深入理解文本的主题意义和叙事意图。

2. 学会运用五五拍戏教学法，合理构建续写框架，确保续写内容逻辑清晰、结构严谨，培养创新能力和情节构建能力。

**学习能力**

1. 通过自评，发现自身的不足并总结改进方法，提升独立学习能力。

2. 通过互评借鉴他人优点，培养团队合作精神。

## 四、教学思路

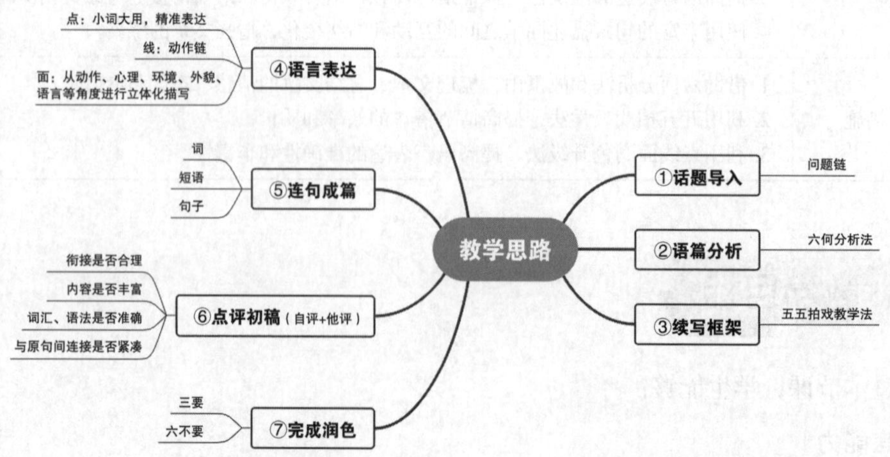

## 五、教学过程

<table>
<tr><th>阶段</th><th>活动形式及步骤</th><th>问题链</th><th>设计意图</th></tr>
<tr><td>话题导入</td><td>结合自己的经历，想象如果自己是后进生，在校园中可能遇到的生活和学习上的困难，并分享自己的感受</td><td>If you were a struggling student, what difficulties would you encounter at school? How would you feel?</td><td>借助问题，引发学生换位思考，体会后进生的困境，激活相关背景知识</td></tr>
<tr><td rowspan="3">语篇分析</td><td>1. 使用六何分析法梳理文本的浅层信息（where/when/who）<br>语篇分析<br>① When Dr. Henderson was assigning（指定）project mates for his psychology class, I secretly hoped he would pair me with my best friend or at least a classmate I could have some fun with. Above all, I hoped he wouldn't assign me to work with the fiercely competitive, extremely serious fellow who always wore dark clothes and apparently had a personality to match. As fate（命运）would have it, Dr. Henderson very deliberately matched everyone in class and announced that I would be working with the one person in class I wanted to avoid.<br>④ With colder weather setting in, our thoughts turned to the upcoming New Year's Day.<br>六何分析法<br>when: When Dr. Henderson was assigning project mates for his psychology class...<br>what: Story mountain<br>where: in the class<br>how: analyze the narrative perspective and style<br>who: Dr. Henderson, I, the fiercely competitive, extremely serious fellow<br>why: analyze the purpose</td><td>1. When did the story take place?<br>2. Where did the story take place?<br>3. Who were the main characters in the text?</td><td>运用六何分析法，梳理文本的基本要素</td></tr>
<tr><td>2. 小组合作，运用故事山梳理文本的情节线和情感线（what）<br>情节分析——story mountain【what】<br>Para. 1:<br>• Dr. Henderson assigned me to work with the guy I wanted to avoid for the project.<br>• unwilling<br>Para. 2–3:<br>• I introduced myself but he ignored me.<br>• cautious<br>Para. 4–5:<br>• I wanted to drop at one point, but I stuck to it.<br>• determined<br>Para. 6:<br>• We decided to study on the psychological well-being of teenagers, but I wasn't sure what it meant exactly.<br>• uncertain<br>续写：<br>• Was our profect completed?<br>• A happy ending?</td><td>1. What was the beginning of the story?<br>2. How did the story develop?<br>3. What was the main conflict of the story?<br>4. What was the resolution of the conflict?<br>5. What was the ending of the story?<br>6. How did the characters' feelings change?</td><td>运用故事山梳理情节线和情感线，进一步把握文本的主要情节和人物的情绪变化</td></tr>
<tr><td>3. 小组组员共同标记有关人物描写的句子，分析文本中主要角色的性格（who）<br>人物分析【who】<br>I<br>• I tried to make the best of it and didn't say anything for fear that I would make things worse.<br>• I actually wanted to drop the class at one point, but stopped short because I didn't want to give him the satisfaction of my chickening out. I decided to stick to it no matter what.<br>I was cautious, determined and ambitious.<br>my teammate<br>• He looked at me as though I weren't there. I felt he treated me as though I would hold him back and probably make him fail to get an A in the course. He wasn't mean or abusive. He just gave me the impression he could do whatever project we dreamed up better if he did it alone.<br>My teammate was indifferent, somewhat cynical, and pursued perfection.</td><td>1. Which sentences can show the characters' personalities?<br>2. Can you conclude the characters' personalities?</td><td>通过标记描写人物性格的句子，分析人物性格，确保续写内容走向不偏离人物特征</td></tr>
</table>

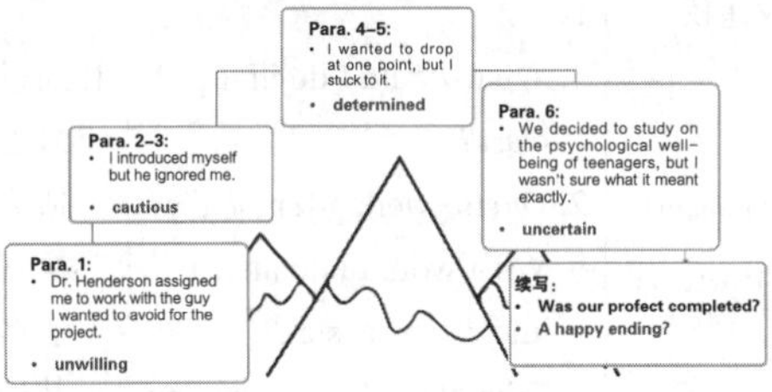

续表

| 阶段 | 活动形式及步骤 | 问题链 | 设计意图 |
| --- | --- | --- | --- |
| 语篇分析 | 4. 分析文本的叙述视角和语言风格（how）<br>**叙述视角与语言风格分析【how】**<br>Narrative perspective<br>• ...I secretly hoped he would pair me with my best friend or at least a classmate I could have some fun with. .<br>第一人称视角：I<br>Narrative style<br>• I went up to my new teammate and introduced myself...<br>• I felt he treated me as though I would hold him back and probably make him fail to get an A in the course.<br>• I wasn't sure what it meant exactly, but at least we had a topic.<br>语言风格 :conversational, straightforward | 1. What is the narrative perspective of the story?<br>2. What is the narrative style of the story? | 梳理文本的叙述视角与语言风格，确保续写内容与原文协同 |
| | 5. 小组讨论语篇所要传达的情感、态度和价值观（why）<br>**情感、态度、价值观分析【why】**<br>人与社会<br>Learn to cooperate.<br>人与自我<br>Cooperation makes perfect. | What values or life perspectives do you think the author wants to convey to readers through the story? | 总结文本的价值观，确保故事结尾的导向正确 |
| 续写框架 | 使用五五拍戏教学法构建一个续写框架（每个段落都续写五个句子，两段续写句子的编号为1—10），并结合情节续写，从承上启下、故事结局和情感、态度和价值观等角度，提供拍戏建议<br>Tip 1：确定演员<br>Tip 2：确定出场顺序<br>**续写框架：五五拍戏教学法**　Tip 1：确定演员　Tip 2：确定出场顺序<br>**Para. 1:** We started to meet regularly to draw up our plans.<br>承上　演员：my teammate & I<br>① I: 做了充足的准备，但不敢发言<br>⑥ My teammate: 开始接受我<br>⑦ My teammate &I: 开始真正的合作<br>⑧ 合作的过程<br>② 合作到了最后一步<br>启下<br>**Para. 2:** One day I got word that he was admitted to hospital for a serious disease.<br>承上　演员：my teammate & I<br>③ I: 去医院看望，同意完成后期工作<br>⑨ I: 得知结果，得到 A<br>⑩ My teammate: 开心<br>④ My teammate &I: 成为好朋友<br>⑤ 这次经历在我们间创造了一种联结<br>故事结局<br>情感、态度、价值观升华 | Part 1:<br>What were the main characters in Para.1 and 2?<br>Part 2:<br>1. What would I do in the class?<br>2. Did the work go smoothly?<br>3. What would I do after I knew he was sick?<br>4. What would be the ending of the story?<br>5. What values or life lessons does the story convey?<br>6. What was my teammate's response?<br>7. What would happen between us?<br>8. What was the process of the cooperation?<br>9. What would be the result of our project?<br>10. How would my teammate feel? | 1. 通过头脑风暴，激发学生的创造力和想象力，探索故事发展的多种可能性并最终选定符合故事发展的结局<br>2. 引导学生借助五五拍戏教学法，构建续写故事情节框架，确保续写内容不偏离原文 |

续表

| 阶段 | 活动形式及步骤 | 问题链 | 设计意图 |
| --- | --- | --- | --- |
| 语言表达 | 1. 根据构思的情节，撰写续写草稿<br>**语言表达：列草稿**<br>**Para. 1:** We started to meet regularly to draw up our plans.<br>I: 做了充足的准备，但不敢发言 — I was afraid to share my opinions although I had made full preparations.<br>My teammate: 开始接受我 — He started to accept my ideas.<br>My teammate &I: 开始真正的合作 — We cooperated with each other.<br>合作的过程 — The project went smoothly as expected.<br>合作到了最后一步 — Our project came to the last stage.<br>2. 教师示范讲解点线面润色升级法，引导学生润色草稿<br>**语言表达：升级表达**<br>We cooperated with each other.<br>Sensing that I could make a contribution to the project, he began to treat me as his partner. With time going by, we gradually cooperated with each other.<br>【微场景：描写合作情况】面：增加动作链 升级思路：增加背景信息<br>The project went smoothly as expected.<br>We developed a hypothesis, set up an experiment to test the hypothesis, ran the tests and did the statistical analysis. The project went smoothly as expected.<br>【微场景：描写项目进展】线：增加动作链 升级思路：举例子<br>Our project came to the last stage.<br>Our project came to the last stage. Wild with joy, we looked forward to the project with confidence of winning an A.<br>【微场景：描写项目结束】面：加心理描写 | 1. Could you use simple sentences to write your draft?<br>2. What do you learn from these sentence patterns?<br>3. How can you use these sentence patterns to improve your sentences? | 1. 引导学生模仿文本的目标语言和句式结构<br>2. 提供升级方法和具体的句型公式，降低后续的写作难度 |
| 连句成篇 | 3. 以“词→短语→句子”循序渐进的方式将润色的十句话连句成篇，从而完成初稿<br>**连句成篇**<br>**请注意连接成分，并进行分类。**<br>连接成分：词 ⑧；短语 ①②③④⑤⑥⑦<br>Paragraph 1: We started to meet regularly to draw up our plans. ① Despite my thorough preparations, I initially hesitated to voice my opinions. But I didn't give up. ② After three regular meetings, he started to consider my ideas with genuine attention. ③ Recognizing my potential contributions, he began to treat me more as an equal partner. We gradually started working well together, and the project went as smoothly as expected. ④ Filled with enthusiasm, we anticipated the project's success with confidence.<br>Paragraph 2: One day I got word that he was admitted to hospital for a serious disease. ⑤ Upon hearing this, I immediately visited him at the hospital, where he asked me to complete our project on my own. I agreed without hesitation. ⑥ During the following days, I worked on the project day and night, ensuring every detail was perfect. Then the big day arrived—we received an A, and I eagerly shared the news with him. ⑦ Much to my joy, he grinned from ear to ear with tears welling up. For us, this experience didn't just complete a project; ⑧ instead, it built a lasting bond that went beyond the cooperation. | Could you use some linking words, phrases or sentences to polish your writing? | 借助连句成篇的技巧，完成续写，确保续写内容的连贯 |
| 评价反馈 | 1. 参照读后续写评价标准，小组成员共同审阅初稿并推选出组内最佳习作<br>2. 各组轮流展示组内成员的最佳习作并简述创作思路<br>3. 教师从情节构思、情感表达和语言运用方面评价学生习作 | 1. Based on the evaluation criteria, what useful advice would you give to your peers?<br>2. Can you choose one of the best works in your group and present it? | 1. 依据读后续写评价标准共同审阅初稿，提高学生的批判性思维和合作能力<br>2. 推选最佳习作，激励学生提升写作质量<br>3. 通过教师点评，引导学生从情节构思、情感表达和语言运用方面提升写作能力 |

续表

| 阶段 | 活动形式及步骤 | 问题链 | 设计意图 |
|---|---|---|---|
| 总结反思 | 总结在创作过程中的收获和遇到的困难，反思在学习和生活中与同学的关系 | 1. What have you learnt today?<br>2. How could you get along with your classmates in the future? | 引导学生更好地理解自己在写作和团队协作中的得失，反思人际关系，并促进其在学习和生活中更好地处理与同学的关系 |
| 作业布置 | 基于师生的评价反馈润色习作 | | 巩固课堂所学，引导学生通过修改润色提升写作质量，提高续写技能 |

## 附录 1：真题文本

① When Dr. Henderson was assigning project mates for his psychology class, I secretly hoped he would pair me with my best friend or at least a classmate I could have some fun with. Above all, I hoped he wouldn't assign me to work with the intense, fiercely competitive, singularly serious fellow who always wore dark clothes and apparently had a personality to match. As fate would have it, Dr. Henderson very deliberately matched everyone in class and announced that I would be working with the one person in class I wanted to avoid.

② I went up to my new teammate and introduced myself. He looked at me as though I weren't there. I felt he treated me as though I would hold him back and probably cause his grade-point average to take a nosedive. He wasn't outright mean or abusive. He just gave me the impression he could do whatever project we dreamed up better if he did it alone.

③ Needless to say, I didn't look forward to an entire term of being brushed off, but I tried to make the best of it and didn't say anything, lest I make things worse.

④ The project required each lab team to develop a hypothesis, set up an experiment to test the hypothesis, run the tests, do the statistical analysis and present the findings. Whatever grade the team received would be shared by both students.

⑤ When my teammate and I met to discuss our project, I was uneasy. Here was this challenging student who had a reputation for single-mindedness and good grades, the exact opposite of me. I was outmatched. I actually wanted to drop the class at one point, but stopped short because I didn't want to give him the satisfaction of my chickening out.

⑥ After lengthy discussions, we somehow agreed to do a study on the tactile-kinesthetic perception of space. I wasn't sure what it meant, but at least we had a topic.

注意

1. 续写词数应为 150 个左右；

2. 请按如下格式在答题卡的相应位置作答。

We started to meet regularly to draw up our plans.__________________________________

____________________________________________________________________________

One day I got word that he was admitted to hospital for a serious disease. ________________

____________________________________________________________________________

附录 2：参考范文

**We started to meet regularly to draw up our plans.** Despite my thorough preparations, I initially hesitated to voice my opinions. But I didn't give up. After three regular meetings, he started to consider my ideas with genuine attention. Recognizing my potential contributions, he began to treat me more as an equal partner. We gradually started working well together, and the project went as smoothly as expected. Filled with enthusiasm, we anticipated the project's success with confidence.

**One day I got word that he was admitted to hospital for a serious disease.** Upon hearing this, I immediately visited him at the hospital, where he asked me to complete our project on my own. I agreed without hesitation. During the following days, I worked on the project day and night, ensuring that every detail was perfect. Then the big day arrived—we received an A, and I eagerly shared the news with him. Much to my joy, he grinned from ear to ear with tears welling up. For us, this experience didn't just complete a project; it also built a lasting bond that went beyond the cooperation.

# 第七节

## 以 2021 年新高考 I / II 卷为例的读后续写教学设计案例

### 一、文本分析

**What** 本文的主题语境是“人与社会”，涉及“良好的人际关系与社会交往”内容。故事讲述一对双胞胎 Jeff 和 Jenna 在母亲节当天亲手为母亲做早餐的暖心故事。在制作烤吐司和鸡肉粥的过程中，他们遇到了诸多挑战，如面包烧焦、粥溢出和 Jeff 烫伤等。

续写第一段的段首句：当孩子们正感到失望时，他们的父亲出现了。

续写第二段的段首句：双胞胎端着早餐上楼叫妈妈起床。

根据续写两段的首句内容，可以推测后面的故事情节：在父亲的帮助下，孩子们成功地为母亲准备了母亲节早餐。当母亲吃着孩子们精心准备的早餐时，整个房间的氛围很温暖。

**Why** 本文旨在探讨家庭中的亲情关系，突出家庭成员之间相互支持和关爱的重要性。通过这一温馨的场景，引导学生感受家庭的温暖与和谐，从而更加珍视与家人之间的关系。本文不仅展现了家人之间的关爱，也通过孩子们在实践中的失败与反思，展现了他们如何在父母的支持下从挑战中学习和成长。

**How** 故事采用时间顺序的叙述方式，通过第三人称视角详细记录了 Jeff 和 Jenna 准备母亲节早餐的过程。文中融入了丰富的动作细节（如“went down the stairs quietly”“boiled the porridge first”“broke two eggs into a plate and added in some milk”等）和情感描写（如“filled with excitement”“how pleased and proud”等），使得故事情节生动而富有感染力。此外，故事中穿插的挑战和解决问题的过程也展示了孩子们的成长和自主能力，增强了故事的教育意义和互动性。

## 二、学情分析

**基本信息：高一学生，班级人数：52 人；平均分：105 分左右；读后续写平均分：12 分左右。**

| 项目 | 内容 |
| --- | --- |
| 已有基础 | 1. 已经了解读后续写这一题型<br>2. 具有基本的读写技能，能按时间顺序或情节发展组织续写内容<br>3. 能够识别文本的主要段落和中心思想<br>4. 能够围绕母亲节主题展开续写，表达对妈妈的感激之情 |
| 存在障碍 | 1. 不能准确梳理出故事的发展情节和主要人物情感变化<br>2. 难以准确把握文本中的转折点或高潮部分，导致续写结构不明晰<br>3. 续写语言贫乏且语法错误较多，很少顾及衔接和过渡，没有句式升级意识<br>4. 不了解读后续写评分标准，也不知道如何进行修改、润色<br>5. 难以将情感融入续写内容，文章缺乏感染力 |
| 发展需求 | 1. 梳理语篇情节发展和主要人物的情感变化<br>2. 构建合理的续写框架，合理升华主题<br>3. 提升语言表达技能，确保语言准确生动，兼顾衔接和过渡<br>4. 熟悉续写评价要点<br>5. 学会用生动的语言提高情感表达能力，使续写内容更加真实感人 |
| 解决措施 | 1. 借助六何分析法分析语篇，精准把握故事核心要素和人物情感变化<br>2. 借助五五拍戏教学法，构建合理续写框架，丰富情节和内容<br>3. 运用点线面润色升级法和连句成篇技巧，提升语言表达<br>4. 借助精细化评价标准，开展针对性润色修改<br>5. 指导学生如何将情感融入续写内容，并通过具体事例展现对妈妈的爱 |

## 三、教学目标

通过本节课，学生能够：

**语言能力**

1. 理解并运用描述动作和人物情感的词汇和句式，增强语言的情感表现力。

2. 模仿故事中的人物语言风格，灵活运用不同句式和表达方式，提升根据情境调整语言的能力。

3. 学会运用点线面润色法提升语言表达能力，掌握连句成篇技巧，增强文章的连贯性和丰富性。

**文化意识**

1. 通过分析双胞胎为母亲准备早餐的故事，感受家庭文化中的关爱与亲情，并理解家庭成员之间互动与支持的重要性。

2. 通过父母与孩子的合作，认识到亲情与支持在成长中的意义，以及如何通过行动表达对家人的关爱。

**思维品质**

1. 学会运用六何分析法，提取故事中的核心要素，分析人物、情节和情感变化，培养批判性思维。

2. 运用五五拍戏教学法合理组织故事情节和人物安排，培养逻辑思维和创造性问题解决能力。

3. 学会运用点线面润色升级法提升语言表达能力，掌握连句成篇技巧，增强文章的连贯性和丰富性。

**学习能力**

1. 通过自评和互评，依据评价标准润色修改自己的写作，提高自主学习能力。

2. 通过同伴互评，培养探究精神，提升合作学习的能力。

## 四、教学思路

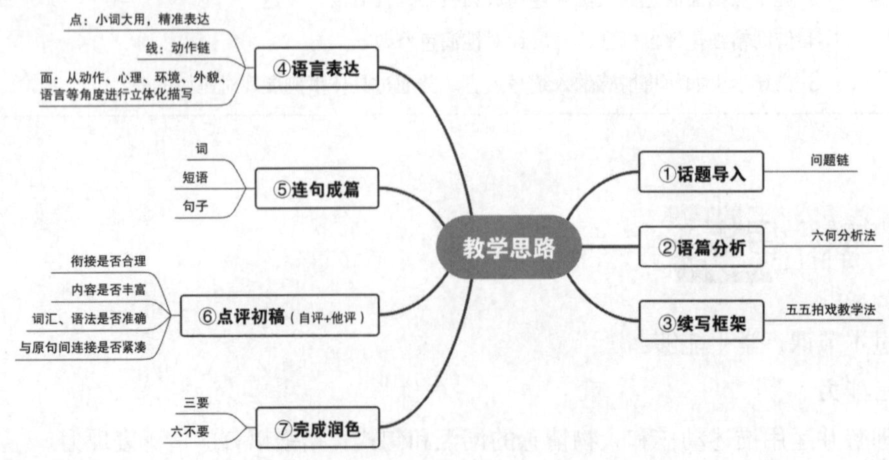

## 五、教学过程

<table>
<tr><th>阶段</th><th>活动形式及步骤</th><th>问题链</th><th>设计意图</th></tr>
<tr><td>话题导入</td><td>1. 母亲节的意义是什么？<br>2. 你曾经为妈妈准备过什么样的母亲节礼物？</td><td>1. What is the meaning of Mother's Day?<br>2. What kind of gift have you ever prepared for your mother?</td><td>借助与学生生活息息相关的问题，引导学生思考母亲节的意义，为后续阅读做铺垫</td></tr>
<tr><td rowspan="3">语篇分析</td><td>1. 快速浏览文章，按照六何分析法提取文章的三要素（when/where/who）<br><br>语篇分析<br>① The twins were filled with excitement as they thought of the surprise they were planning for Mother's Day. How pleased and proud Mother would be when they brought her breakfast in bed. They planned to make French toast and chicken porridge. They had watched their mother in the kitchen. There was nothing to it. Jenna and Jeff knew exactly what to do.<br>④ As the twins looked around them in disappointment, their father appeared.<br>⑤ The twins carried the breakfast upstairs and woke their mother up.<br><br>六何分析法<br>when: Mother's Day<br>where: in the kitchen<br>who: Twins (Jenna and Jeff), Mother, Father<br>what: Story mountain<br>how: analyze the narrative perspective and style<br>why: analyze the purpose</td><td>1. When did the story take place?<br>2. Where did the story take place?<br>3. Who were the key characters in the text?</td><td>运用六何分析法，梳理语篇的基本要素</td></tr>
<tr><td>2. 运用故事山梳理故事情节及其主要人物的情感态度变化（what）<br><br>情节分析——story mountain【what】<br>Para. 1:<br>• The twins eagerly planned a Mother's Day surprise, imagining their mother's joy.<br>• twins: excited<br>Para. 2:<br>• the twins struggled in the kitchen but persevered with their breakfast preparation.<br>• twins:optimistic and confident<br>Para. 3:<br>• The twins faced many cooking challenges,making a mess in the kitchen.<br>• twins:panicked, calm, disappointed<br>续写：<br>• Their father appeared...<br>• twins:delighted<br>续写：<br>• They woke their mother up...<br>• A happy ending?</td><td>1. What was the beginning of the story?<br>2. How did the story develop?<br>3. What was the main conflict of the story?<br>4. What was the resolution of the conflict?<br>5. What was the ending of the story?<br>6. How did the twins' feelings change?</td><td>运用故事山梳理文章的情节、情感两条线，引导学生关注故事走向和情感变化</td></tr>
<tr><td>3. 标记出文本中有关主要人物的描写和介绍，进行人物分析 (who)<br><br>人物分析【who】<br>Jenna<br>• Jenna threw the burnt piece into the sink and put in the other slice of bread. This time, she turned down the fire so it cooked nicely.<br>• Jenna panicked.<br>Jenna was determined, diligent, and adaptable.<br><br>Jeff<br>• Thankfully, Jeff stayed calm and turned off the gas quickly.<br>• But Jeff's hand touched the hot burner, and he gave a cry of pain.<br>Jeff was calm, decisive, and responsive.</td><td>1. Which sentences can show the characters' personalities?<br>2. Can you conclude the characters' personalities?</td><td>关注故事主要人物的描写和分析，确保续写故事走向不偏离人物特征</td></tr>
</table>

续表

| 阶段 | 活动形式及步骤 | 问题链 | 设计意图 |
| --- | --- | --- | --- |
| 语篇分析 | 4. 分析叙述视角和语言风格（how）<br>**叙述视角与语言风格分析【How】**<br>Narrative perspective<br>• The twins were filled with excitement...<br>• They planned to make...<br>• Jenna and Jeff knew exactly what to do...<br>第三人称视角：They, the twins<br>Narrative style<br>• ...went down the stairs quietly... boiled the porridge first...broke two eggs into a plate and added in some milk...<br>• ...filled with excitement...<br>• ...how pleased and proud...<br>语言风格：descriptive，lively，emotional | 1. What are the narrative perspective and narrative style of this story?<br>2. Can you give some examples? | 引导学生分析文本的叙述视角和语言风格，确保续写的语言协同 |
| | 5. 提炼分析文本的情感、态度和价值观 (why)<br>**情感、态度、价值观分析【why】**<br>人与社会<br>Explore the family affection, and experience the warm and harmonious family life. | 1. What does the author want to convey?<br>2. What is the most important aspect of family affection?<br>3. How do you understand "warm and harmonious family life"? | 引导学生深入思考故事中蕴含的情感、态度、价值观，进一步理解作者的意图，提升学生对亲情的理解 |
| 续写框架 | 使用五五拍戏教学法构建一个续写框架（每个段落都续写五个句子，两段续写句子的编号为 1—10），并结合情节续写，从承上启下、故事结局和情感、态度和价值观等角度，提供拍戏建议<br>Tip 1：确定演员<br>Tip 2：确定出场顺序<br>**续写框架：五五拍戏教学法**　Tip 1：确定演员　Tip 2：确定出场顺序<br>**Para. 1:** As the twins looked around them in disappointment, their father appeared.<br>承上　演员：twins & their father<br>① father: 生气询问发生了什么<br>⑥ twins: 想要为妈妈准备早餐<br>⑦ father: 缓和语气，并帮忙<br>⑧ twins and father: 完成了早餐<br>② twins: 他们期待把早餐端给妈妈<br>启下<br>**Para. 2:** The twins carried the breakfast upstairs and woke their mother up.<br>承上　演员：twins& their father and mother<br>③ twins 说：母亲节快乐！ father 附和着<br>⑨ mother：看到早餐<br>⑩ mother: 从未想过会有这顿早餐　故事结局<br>④ mother: 吃早餐<br>⑤ 房间充满了幸福与温暖<br>情感、态度、价值观升华 | Part 1:<br>What were the main characters in Para.1 and 2?<br>Part 2:<br>1. How did their father feel upon seeing the mess in the kitchen?<br>2. How did the twins feel when they finished cooking the breakfast?<br>3. What did the twins do after waking their mother up?<br>4. What would be the ending of the story?<br>5. What was the atmosphere in the room at that moment, and why?<br>6. How did the twins react to their father's reaction?<br>7. What did their father do to help them?<br>8. What did the twins do under their father's help?<br>9. How did their mother react?<br>10. How did their mother feel? | 提供清晰的续写框架，引导学生构建合理的故事情节 |

续表

| 阶段 | 活动形式及步骤 | 问题链 | 设计意图 |
| --- | --- | --- | --- |
| 语言表达 | 1. 结合续写框架，撰写草稿<br>**语言表达：列草稿**<br>**Para.1:** As the twins looked around them in disappointment, their father appeared.<br>father: 生气询问发生了什么 — Their father angrily asked what had happened.<br>twins: 想要为妈妈准备早餐 — The twins said they wanted to give their mother a surprise.<br>father: 缓和语气，并帮忙 — Their father softened his tone and helped them.<br>twins and father: 完成了早餐 — They completed the breakfast.<br>twins: 他们期待把早餐端给妈妈 — They were eager to present the breakfast to Mom.<br>2. 教师示例讲解点线面润色升级法，并进行相应的微技能训练<br>**语言表达微技能：点线面润色升级法** <br>点：具体的某个动作<br>线：将动作进行拆解形成一条动作链<br>面：多面立体化 外貌描写 环境描写 语言描写 心理描写<br>3. 润色草稿，并梳理升级思路<br>**语言表达：升级表达**<br>**Para. 1:** As the twins looked around them in disappointment, their father appeared.<br>说明：为了突出思路，每个句子都做了升级。考试时并不需要每个句子都进行升级。<br>Their father asked what had happened<br>Upon seeing the mess in the kitchen, his eyes flashed with anger as he yelled, "What are you doing?<br>微场景：表示惊讶和生气<br>面：场景描写（介词短语）<br>The twins said they wanted to give their mother a surprise.<br>The twins hung their heads in embarrassment and murmured, "We just want to give mom a surprise."<br>微场景：表示尴尬和委屈<br>点：细节动词<br>线：动作链（状语）<br>面：语言描写（直接引语） | 1. What would you do to polish your draft?<br>2. Can you conclude the tips to polish your writing? | 通过点线面润色升级法，帮助学生提高写作表达水平，使表达更加精准、丰富 |
| 连句成篇 | 以"词→短语→句子"循序渐进的方式将润色的十句话连句成篇，完成初稿<br>**连句成篇**<br>连接成分：连词 ⑥；短语 ①②③④⑦；句子 ⑤<br>**Paragraph 1:** As the twins looked around them in disappointment, their father appeared. ① Upon seeing the mess in the kitchen, his eyes flashed with anger as he yelled, "What are you doing?" The twins hung their heads in embarrassment and murmured "We just want to give Mom a surprise." ② Sensing the children's shame, he softened his tone and added, "Alright. Let's do it together." ③ Under their father's patient guidance, they quickly cleaned up the kitchen, skillfully fried the remaining bread and well boiled the porridge. With everything ready, they were eager to present the meal to Mom.<br>**Paragraph 2:** The twins carried the breakfast upstairs and woke their mother up. "Happy Mother's Day, Mom!" They exclaimed excitedly. "Just for you!" their father said with a smile. ④ Amazed at the breakfast — freshly cooked toast and steaming porridge,their mother widened eyes in great delight. ⑤ Never had she imagined that there would be such a heartwarming surprise awaiting her. ⑥ She then picked up a piece of toast, took a big bite of it and said, "This is the best breakfast I've ever tasted." ⑦ At that moment, sunlight gently filled the entire bedroom, bathing every corner with an overflowing sense of happiness and warmth. | How do you put the following sentences together? | 运用"词→短语→句子"的方法，使语言衔接更加有序 |
| 点评初稿 | 结合评价量表进行自评和互评【详见附录一及附录二】 | Based on the evaluation criteria, what useful advice would you give to your peers? | 提供详细的评分标准，使学生在创作时更具针对性，牢记评价要点 |

续表

| 阶段 | 活动形式及步骤 | 问题链 | 设计意图 |
|---|---|---|---|
| 润色习作 | 结合评价反馈润色自己的习作 | How could you refine your writing based on the feedback? | 结合同伴反馈，润色并完善写作内容 |

## 附录 1：真题文本

① The twins were filled with excitement as they thought of the surprise they were planning for Mother's Day. How pleased and proud Mother would be when they brought her breakfast in bed. They planned to make French toast and chicken porridge. They had watched their mother in the kitchen. There was nothing to it. Jenna and Jeff knew exactly what to do.

② The big day came at last. The alarm rang at 6 a.m. The pair went down the stairs quietly to the kitchen. They decided to boil the porridge first. They put some rice into a pot of water and left it to boil while they made the French toast. Jeff broke two eggs into a plate and added in some milk. Jenna found the bread and put two slices into the egg mixture. Next, Jeff turned on the second stove burner to heat up the frying pan. Everything was going smoothly until Jeff started frying the bread. The pan was too hot and the bread turned black within seconds. Jenna threw the burnt piece into the sink and put in the other slice of bread. This time, she turned down the fire so it cooked nicely.

③ Then Jeff noticed steam shooting out of the pot and the lid starting to shake. The next minute, the porridge boiled over and put out the fire. Jenna panicked. Thankfully, Jeff stayed calm and turned off the gas quickly. But the stove was a mess now. Jenna told Jeff to clean it up so they could continue to cook the rest of the porridge. But Jeff's hand touched the hot burner and he gave a cry of pain. Jenna made him put his hand in cold water. Then she caught the smell of burning. Oh dear! The piece of bread in the pan had turned black as well.

### 注意

1. 续写词数应为 150 个左右；

2. 请按如下格式在答题卡的相应位置作答。

As the twins looked around them in disappointment, their father appeared. ______________

________________________________________________________________________

The twins carried the breakfast upstairs and woke their mother up. ____________________

________________________________________________________________________

附录2：参考范文

**As the twins looked around them in disappointment, their father appeared.** Upon seeing the mess in the kitchen, his eyes flashed with anger as he yelled, "What are you doing?" The twins hung their heads in embarrassment and murmured, "We just want to give Mom a surprise." Sensing the children's shame, he softened his tone and added, "Alright. Let's do it together." Under their father's patient guidance, they quickly cleaned up the kitchen, skillfully fried the remaining bread and well boiled the porridge. With everything ready, they were eager to present the meal to Mom.

**The twins carried the breakfast upstairs and woke their mother up.** "Happy Mother's Day, Mom!" They exclaimed excitedly. "Just for you!" their father said with a smile. Amazed at the breakfast—freshly cooked toast and steaming porridge, their mother widened eyes in great delight. Never had she imagined that there would be such a heartwarming surprise awaiting her. She then picked up a piece of toast, took a big bite of it and said, "This is the best breakfast I've ever tasted." At that moment, sunlight gently filled the entire bedroom, bathing every corner with an overflowing sense of happiness and warmth.

# 第八节

# 以 2020 年新高考全国 I 卷为例的读后续写教学设计案例

## 一、文本分析

**What** 本文涉及“人与社会”和“人与自我”双重主题语境。故事发生在一个充满爱的社区。Mrs. Meredith 是社区里最具爱心的人，经常帮助那些有需要的人，其中包括 Bernard 一家。当得知 Bernard 想自己努力赚钱以减轻家庭负担后，Mrs. Meredith 带领她的三个孩子一起想办法帮助 Bernard 实现愿望。

续写第一段的段首句：Mrs. Meredith 听了 John 的想法，她也认为这个想法很不错。

续写第二段的段首句：一切都准备好了，Bernard 开始了他的新生意。

根据续写两段的段首句内容，可以预测后面的故事情节：在 Mrs. Meredith 一家的帮助和鼓励下，Bernard 在社区卖爆米花赚了他人生中的第一笔钱，这不仅缓解了家里的经济困难，也让他深切感受到社区成员的关心与支持。

**Why** 本文通过描写 Mrs. Meredith 一家积极帮助 Bernard 的过程，展示了人与人之间的善意和社区人员之间的相互支持。通过他们的善举，传达了积极的价值观：帮助他人的同时也会获得快乐，并实现人生的意义和价值。

**How** 故事采用第三人称进行叙述，通过简洁生动的语言和细腻的动作描写，鲜明地展现了人物的内心世界和情感变化。通过生动的对话和细致的情节描写，人物的性格得以凸显，情感的波动也更加清晰。故事情节紧凑，层层推进，引导读者产生情感共鸣，并进一步强调了帮助他人所带来的意义和价值。

## 二、学情分析

**基本信息：高一文科班学生，班级人数：54 人；平均分：90 分左右，读后续写平均分：12 分左右。**

| 项目 | 内容 |
|---|---|
| 已有基础 | 1. 能够获取记叙文六要素等基本信息<br>2. 具备基本的写作能力<br>3. 懂得助人为乐的意义 |
| 存在障碍 | 1. 不能准确梳理故事中人物的情感变化<br>2. 难以构建出新颖、合理的情节<br>3. 续写词汇匮乏、句式单一<br>4. 续写内容、语言风格、逻辑与原文不协同<br>5. 不了解读后续写评分标准 |
| 发展需求 | 1. 准确梳理故事情节，合理构思续写情节，使其符合逻辑<br>2. 掌握如何使续写内容与原文紧密衔接、如何塑造生动的人物形象等技巧<br>3. 积累与描述人物、情感和动作等相关的词汇和表达<br>4. 丰富续写内容，保持语言风格与原文一致<br>5. 了解读后续写评分标准<br>6. 理解人与人之间的善意带来的温暖与支持，以及为个人和社会所带来的价值和意义 |
| 解决措施 | 1. 运用六何分析法解读文本，深入理解文本内容，为后续续写奠定基础<br>2. 采用五五拍戏教学法构建清晰的故事框架<br>3. 运用点线面润色升级法，从动作点出发，逐步扩展成动作链，并注重对人物内心、外貌、情节和环境等方面的升级和润色，使续写内容更加丰富、生动<br>4. 使用恰当的衔接手段，使续写内容衔接流畅，增强整体的连贯性<br>5. 借助读后续写评价标准和“三要六不要”原则，做到会润色也会赏析<br>6. 结合自己的经历讨论助人与受助对个人和社会的意义 |

## 三、教学目标

通过本节课，学生能够：

**语言能力**

1. 理解并运用动词短语描绘人物在困难环境中努力奋斗的状态和人物突然站起时的活力与决心，传递情节的动态感与紧张感。

2. 通过学习虚拟语气表达人物的遗憾与对美好愿望的向往，更好地理解人物的心理变化。

3. 赏析文章的简洁叙事风格，学会使用直接对话和动作描写来展现人物性格与情节发展。

**文化意识**

理解并尊重不同群体之间的差异，认识到社区成员内相互支持和帮助的重要性，并体会到关爱他人和奉献精神在社会中的价值。

**思维品质**

1. 运用六何分析法，批判性地分析文本中的人物、情节、背景及其相互之间的关系，深入理解文本背后的动机与意义。

2. 运用五五拍戏教学法，有逻辑地构建故事的续写框架，培养情节构建与组织能力。

**学习能力**

1. 在自评过程中，培养独立思考的能力并进行自我修正，提升自主学习的能力。

2. 在同伴互评中，激发探究精神，培养批判性思维和合作学习的能力。

## 四、教学思路

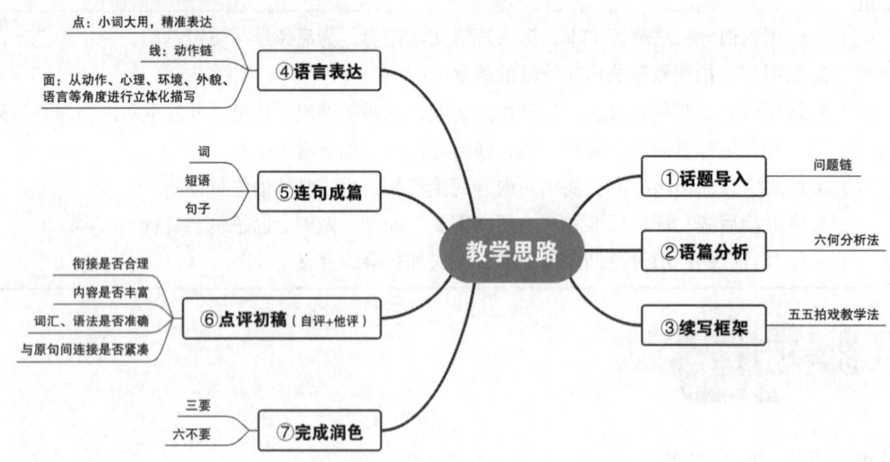

## 五、教学过程

| 阶段 | 活动形式与步骤 | 问题链 | 设计意图 |
| --- | --- | --- | --- |
| 话题导入 | 小组讨论谚语"授人以鱼，不如授人以渔"的内涵 | How do you understand the Chinese proverb, "Give people fish and you feed them for a day; Teach them how to fish and you feed them for a lifetime."？ | 借助汉语谚语引发学生关注助人的意义，并思考帮助人的方式，为后续的阅读奠定基础 |
| 语篇分析 | 1. 借助六何分析法，梳理文本的基本要素<br>**语篇分析**<br>① The Meredith family lived in a small community. As the economy was in decline some people in the town had lost their jobs.<br>③ The little boy—his name was Bernard—had interested her very much.<br>④ "I wish you could see him", she said to her own children, John, Harry and Clara.<br>**六何分析法**<br>when: during the economic decline<br>where: in a small community<br>who: The Meredith family(Mrs. Meredith, John, Harry and Clara), the poor family's little boy—Bernard<br>what: Story mountain<br>how: analyze the narrative perspective and style<br>why: analyze the purpose | 1. When did the story take place?<br>2. Where did the story take place?<br>3. Who were the main characters in the story? | 利用六何分析法，梳理文本浅层信息：when、where、who。厘清故事发生的时空背景和人物关系 |
| | 2. 运用故事山梳理故事情节及其主要人物的情感、态度变化（what）<br>**情节分析——story mountain【what】**<br>Para. 1: Economic decline led to hardships in the Meredith community. Mrs. Meredith: kind , thoughtful, compassionate<br>Para. 2-4: Mrs. Meredith showed compassion by helping the poor. She introduced Bernard to her children. Harry and Clara: sympathetic, supportive John: quick-minded, confident<br>Para. 5-8: The Meredith children devised a plan to help Bernard earn money. Bernard: responsible, determined<br>续写: Mrs. Meredith thought John's idea a good one. Mrs. Meredith: satisfied?<br>续写: Bernard started out on his new business. A happy ending? | 1. What was the beginning of the story?<br>2. How did the story develop?<br>3. What was the main conflict of the story?<br>4. What was the resolution of the conflict?<br>5. What was the ending of the story?<br>6. How did the main characters' feelings change? | 运用故事山梳理文本的情节、情感两条线，引导学生关注故事走向和情感变化 |

续表

| 阶段 | 活动形式与步骤 | 问题链 | 设计意图 |
| --- | --- | --- | --- |
| 语篇分析 | 3. 标记出文本中相关主要人物的描写和介绍，进行人物分析 (who) 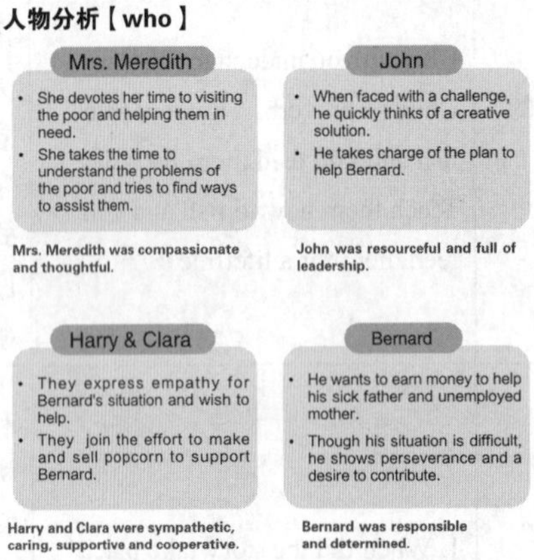<br>人物分析【who】<br>Mrs. Meredith<br>• She devotes her time to visiting the poor and helping them in need.<br>• She takes the time to understand the problems of the poor and tries to find ways to assist them.<br>Mrs. Meredith was compassionate and thoughtful.<br>John<br>• When faced with a challenge, he quickly thinks of a creative solution.<br>• He takes charge of the plan to help Bernard.<br>John was resourceful and full of leadership.<br>Harry & Clara<br>• They express empathy for Bernard's situation and wish to help.<br>• They join the effort to make and sell popcorn to support Bernard.<br>Harry and Clara were sympathetic, caring, supportive and cooperative.<br>Bernard<br>• He wants to earn money to help his sick father and unemployed mother.<br>• Though his situation is difficult, he shows perseverance and a desire to contribute.<br>Bernard was responsible and determined. | 1. Which sentences can show the characters' personalities?<br>2. Could you conclude the characters' personalities? | 关注故事主要人物的描写并进行分析，确保续写内容走向不偏离人物特征 |
| | 4. 分析文本的叙述视角和语言风格（how） 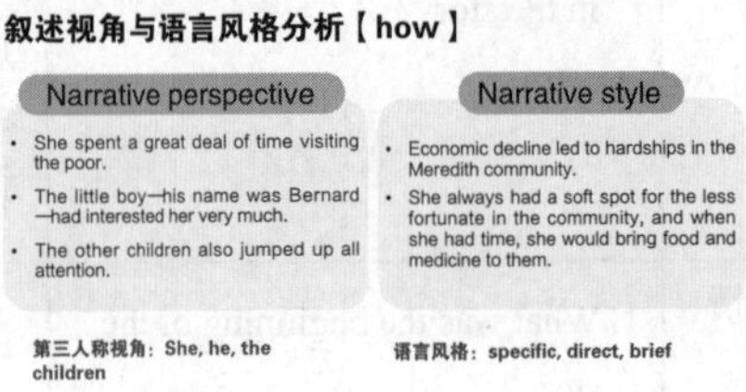<br>叙述视角与语言风格分析【how】<br>Narrative perspective<br>• She spent a great deal of time visiting the poor.<br>• The little boy—his name was Bernard—had interested her very much.<br>• The other children also jumped up all attention.<br>第三人称视角：She, he, the children<br>Narrative style<br>• Economic decline led to hardships in the Meredith community.<br>• She always had a soft spot for the less fortunate in the community, and when she had time, she would bring food and medicine to them.<br>语言风格：specific, direct, brief | 1. What are the narrative perspective and language style of this story?<br>2. Can you give some examples? | 引导学生分析文本的叙述视角和语言风格，确保续写内容的语言与原文协同 |
| | 5. 分析文本的情感、态度和价值观 (why) 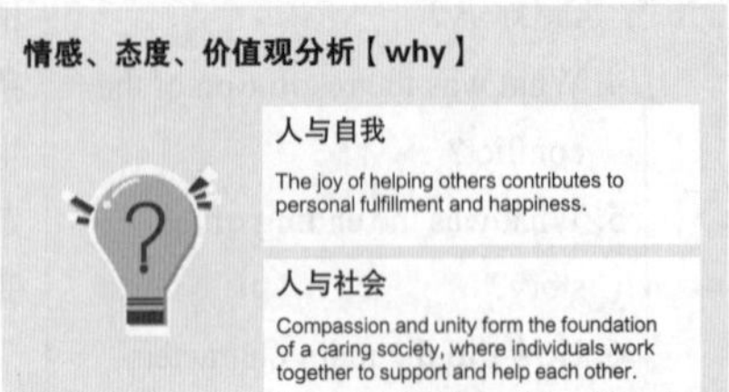<br>情感、态度、价值观分析【why】<br>人与自我<br>The joy of helping others contributes to personal fulfillment and happiness.<br>人与社会<br>Compassion and unity form the foundation of a caring society, where individuals work together to support and help each other. | 1. If you encounter a similar situation, what will you do?<br>2. What can we learn from the story? | 培养学生的爱心，帮助学生树立助人的正确观念，强化其社会责任感 |

续表

| 阶段 | 活动形式与步骤 | 问题链 | 设计意图 |
| --- | --- | --- | --- |
| 续写框架 | 使用五五拍戏教学法构建续写框架（每个段落都续写五个句子，两段续写句子的编号为1—10），并结合情节进行续写，从承上启下、故事结局和情感、态度和价值观等角度，提供拍戏建议<br>Tip 1：确定演员<br>Tip 2：确定出场顺序<br>Tip 3：戏份不够，细节或环境来凑 <br>**续写框架：五五拍戏教学法**<br>Tip 1：确定演员　Tip 2：确定出场顺序<br>**Para. 1:** When Mrs. Meredith heard of John's idea, she thought it was a good one, too.<br>承上　演员：Mrs. Meredith, her children, Bernard<br>Mrs. Meredith：让每个人都开始准备<br>具体分工<br>Tip 3：戏份不够，细节或环境来凑<br>Mrs.Meredith: 带回 Bernard<br>Bernard: 非常感动<br>启下<br>**Para. 2:** With everything ready, Bernard started out on his new business.<br>承上　演员：Bernard, Mrs. Meredith, her children<br>Bernard: 很发愁没什么人买爆米花<br>the Merediths: 他们善意地鼓励他<br>Bernard: 卖掉了所有的爆米花　故事结局<br>Bernard: 感到了来自他人的温暖和善意<br>the Merediths: 帮助别人不仅能照亮别人还能点亮自己<br>情感、态度、价值观升华 | Part 1:<br>What were the main characters in Para. 1 and 2?<br>Part 2:<br>1. What did Mrs.Meredith do with John's idea?<br>2. How did Bernard feel when everything was ready?<br>3.What difficulties did Bernard face when he first started selling the popcorn?<br>4. What was the ending of the story?<br>5. What did they learn from helping others?<br>6. How did the preparations go, and what was the outcome of the porpcorn?<br>7. What did Mrs. Meredith do while the kids were making popcorn?<br>8. How did Mrs. Meredith and her children encourage Bernard?<br>9. Did Bernard sell all the popcorn? | 提供清晰的续写框架，引导学生构建合理的故事情节 |
| 语言表达 | 1. 结合续写框架，撰写草稿 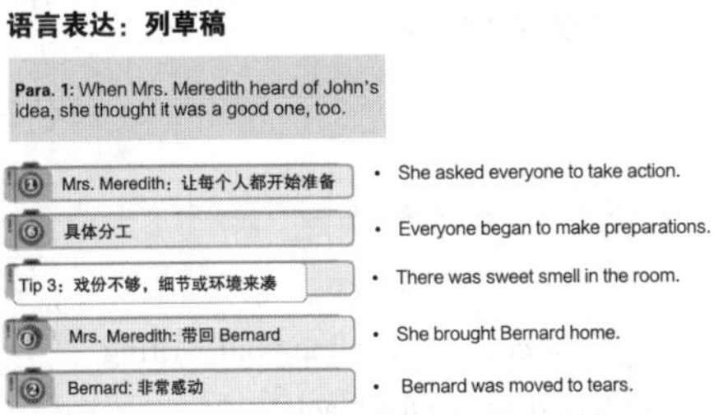<br>**语言表达：列草稿**<br>**Para. 1:** When Mrs. Meredith heard of John's idea, she thought it was a good one, too.<br>Mrs. Meredith：让每个人都开始准备 · She asked everyone to take action.<br>具体分工 · Everyone began to make preparations.<br>Tip 3：戏份不够，细节或环境来凑 · There was sweet smell in the room.<br>Mrs. Meredith: 带回 Bernard · She brought Bernard home.<br>Bernard: 非常感动 · Bernard was moved to tears.<br>2. 教师示例讲解点线面润色升级法，并进行相应的微技能训练 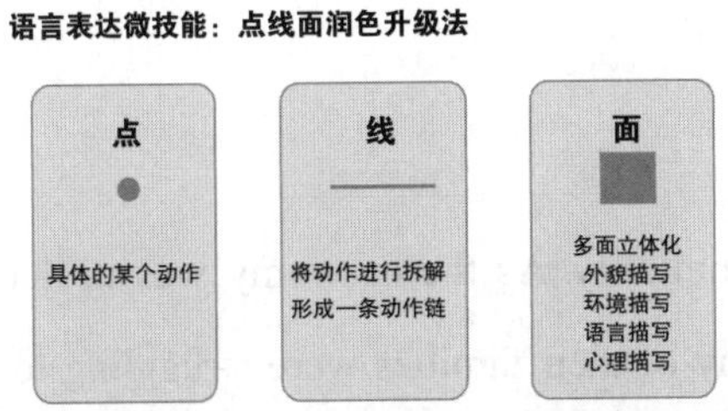<br>**语言表达微技能：点线面润色升级法**<br>点：具体的某个动作<br>线：将动作进行拆解形成一条动作链<br>面：多面立体化 外貌描写 环境描写 语言描写 心理描写 | 1.How would you polish your draft?<br>2.Can you conclude some tips to polish your writing? | 引导学生采用点线面润色升级法，从人物动作链、心理、环境、外貌等多个方面进行描写，以使人物形象更加丰满、立体，提升语言的丰富性和精准度，增强语言表达的感染力 |

续表

| 阶段 | 活动形式与步骤 | 问题链 | 设计意图 |
| --- | --- | --- | --- |
| 语言表达 | 3. 借助点线面润色升级法润色草稿，并标记微场景<br>**语言表达：升级表达**<br>说明：为了突出思路，笔者将每个句子都做了升级。考试时考生不需要升级每个句子<br>**Para.1:**<br>When Mrs. Meredith heard of John's idea, she thought it was a good one, too.<br>She asked everyone to take action.<br>微场景：表示赞同<br>点：精准动词<br>线：动作链（非谓语，不定式）<br>Nodding with smile, she urged everyone to go separate ways to make preparations.<br>Everyone began to make preparations.<br>微场景：具体分工描写<br>线：动作链（连续动词）<br>Mrs.Meredith set off to buy some paper bags, John found out the big box of corn, and the other two began making delicious popcorn. | | |
| 连句成篇 | 利用过渡词、短语、句子使文章通顺、衔接自然<br>**连句成篇**<br>**请注意连接成分，并进行分类。**<br>连接成分：词 ②⑤⑥⑧；短语 ①④⑦⑨；句子 ③<br>**Paragraph 1:** When Mrs. Meredith heard of John's idea, she thought it was a good one, too. ① Nodding with smile, she urged everyone to go separate ways to make preparations. Mrs. Meredith set off to buy some paper bags, John found out a big box of corn, ② and the other two began making delicious popcorn.The following hours witnessed them working busily and very soon the sweet smell of popcorn filled the entire room. ③ When Mrs. Meredith came back, she also brought Bernard with her. ④ Upon seeing the popcorn, Bernard was moved to tears with gratitude. Together, they packed the popcorn into paper bags.<br>**Paragraph 2:** With everything ready, Bernard started out on his new business. ⑤ Initially, for lack of experience, hard as he tried, few people bought his popcorn, leaving him red-faced and with sweat pouring down. ⑥ Fortunately, Mrs. Meredith and her children surrounded him, continuously encouraging him by saying "You can do it! ⑦ With renewed courage, he went from door to door, and ⑧ eventually sold all the popcorn. ⑨ Holding the money, Bernard felt a strong surge of warmth, which came from the kindness and support of the lovely people around him. The Merediths also discovered that not only does lending a helping hand brighten Bernard's day but also lights a spark in themselves. | How can you use transitional words, phrases, and sentence patterns to make your writing smoothly and naturally connected? | 指导学生使用过渡词、短语、句子，增强文章的连贯性 |
| 点评初稿 | 利用评价量表，进行自评和互评【详见附录一及附录二】 | Based on the evaluation criteria, what useful advice would you give to your peers? | 为学生提供明确的写作标准，使其能有针对性地进行自我评估与改进 |
| 润色习作 | 结合评价反馈润色自己的习作 | How could you refine your writing based on the feedback? | 结合同伴反馈，润色、完善写作内容，巩固课堂所学 |

## 附录 1：真题文本

① The Meredith family lived in a small community. As the economy was in decline, some people in the town had lost their jobs. Many of their families were struggling to make ends meet. People were trying to help each other meet the challenges.

② Mrs. Meredith was a most kind and thoughtful woman. She spent a great deal of time visiting the poor. She knew they had problems, and they needed all kinds of help. When she had time, she would bring food and medicine to them.

③ One morning she told her children about a family she had visited the day before. There was a man sick in bed, his wife, who took care of him and could not go out to work, and their little boy. The little boy—his name was Bernard—had interested her very much.

④ "I wish you could see him," she said to her own children, John, Harry and Clara. "He is such a help to his mother. He wants very much to earn some money, but I don't see what he can do."

⑤ After their mother left the room, the children sat thinking about Bernard. "I wish we could help him to earn money," said Clara, "His family is suffering so much."

⑥ "So do I," said Harry, "We really should do something to assist them."

⑦ For some moments, John said nothing, but, suddenly, he sprang to his feet and cried, "I have a great idea! I have a solution that we can all help accomplish (完成)."

⑧ The other children also jumped up all attention. When John had an idea, it was sure to be a good one, "I tell you what we can do," said John. "You know that big box of corn Uncle John sent us? Well, we can make popcorn (爆米花), and put it into paper bags, and Bernard can take it around to the houses and sell it."

**注意**

1. 续写词数应为 150 个左右：
2. 请按如下格式在答题卡的相应位置作答。

When Mrs. Meredith heard of John's idea, she thought it was a good one, too.______________

______________________________________________________________________

With everything ready, Bernard started out on his new business.______________________

______________________________________________________________________

附录2：参考范文

**When Mrs. Meredith heard of John's idea, she thought it was a good one, too.** Nodding with smile, she urged everyone to go separate ways to make preparations. Mrs. Meredith set off to buy some paper bags, John found out the big box of corn, and the other two began making delicious popcorn. The following hours witnessed them working busily and very soon the sweet smell of popcorn filled the entire room. When Mrs. Meredith came back, she also brought Bernard with her. Upon seeing the popcorn, Bernard was moved to tears with gratitude. Together, they packed the popcorn into paper bags.

**With everything ready, Bernard started out on his new business.** Initially, for lack of experience, hard as he tried, few people bought his popcorn, leaving him red-faced and with sweat pouring down . Fortunately, Mrs. Meredith and her children surrounded him, continuously encouraging him by saying, "You can do it!". With renewed courage, he went from door to door, and eventually sold all the popcorn. Holding the money, Bernard felt a strong surge of warmth, which came from the kindness and support of the lovely people around him. The Merediths also discovered that not only does lending a helping hand brighten Bernard's day but also lights a spark in themselves.

# 第九节

## 以 2024 年新高考 I 卷为例的读后续写教学设计案例

### 一、文本分析

**What** 本文的主题语境是“人与社会”和“人与自我”，涉及“良好的人际关系与社会交往”“跨文化沟通、包容与合作”和“优秀品行”等内容。故事讲述了身处异乡的“我”因为飞机延误，深夜抵达维也纳，需要赶最后一班公交车去往布拉格的窘境。为了赶时间，“我”匆忙搭乘了 Gunter 的出租车。尽管语言沟通上遇到了一些障碍，Gunter 还是成功在最后一刻将“我”送到车站，然而这个时候“我”却发现自己没有现金，更糟糕的是取款机也无法使用。

续写第一段的段首句：“我”跑回来告诉 Gunter 这个坏消息。

续写第二段的段首句：四天后，我返回维也纳，如约给 Gunter 打电话。

根据续写两段的段首句内容，可以预测后面的故事情节：“我”如何与 Gunter 交流并处理没有现金付车费的问题并顺利赶上最后一班公交车前往布拉格。“我”返回维也纳后，兑现承诺给 Gunter 打电话联系补付车费事宜。Gunter 相信了我，在后续的重逢里，我感叹正是来自陌生人的友善，让这个世界变得更加美好。

**Why** 本文描述了“我”在国际旅行中因意外状况几乎错过汽车的经历，表达了对生活中出现的不确定性和挑战的理解，同时赞扬了人与人之间的善意和信任。本文描述了在赶车的过程中当地出租车司机 Gunter 表现出的友善和热情，表达了对人性温暖的肯定，呼吁以乐观和互助的态度面对生活的意外。

**How** 故事以第一人称视角及细腻的动作和语言描写，层层展现旅途中遇到的困难与转机，同时展现角色的情感和心理变化，帮助读者深入理解人物性格。例如，“The moment I got off the plane, I ran like crazy through the airport building.”表现出“我”在紧急情况下的焦虑。“I flashed him an apologetic smile as I pulled out my Portuguese bankcard.”体现了“我”在无助时的心存歉意的细腻情感。通过生动活泼的语言，文章让读者身临其境地感受“我”的窘迫，以及从陌生出租车司机 Gunter 那里收获的友善和温暖。

此外，文章还多次出现动作链（如 ① The moment I got off the plane, I ran like crazy through the airport building and jumped into the first taxi on the rank without a second thought. ② Gunter parked the taxi behind the bus, turned around, and looked at me with a big smile on his face. ③ I jumped out of the car, made a mad run for the machine, and popped my card in, only to read the message: “Out of order. Sorry.”）。这些动作链既增强了故事的可读性，也精准地传递了人物在面临窘境时焦急和无助的心理活动。

在刻画人物的时候本文使用了拟人和比喻等修辞手法。例如 When I was about to give up, Gunter fished out his little phone and rang up a friend. 生动形象地描绘了 Gunter 从容且热心的动作，增加了人物的亲切感。而“A feeling of helplessness washed over me as I saw the bus queue thinning out”中的“thin out”形象地表现了公交车即将开走前的情境，侧面表现了人物的焦急心理，反衬了 Gunter 对我的信任的难能可贵，凸显了文章的互助主题。

## 二、学情分析

**基本信息：高三学生，班级人数：48 人；平均分：105 分左右；读后续写平均分：15 分左右。**

| 项目 | 内容 |
| --- | --- |
| 已有基础 | 1. 能使用故事山梳理故事的基本情节，梳理 when、where 和 who 信息<br>2. 会利用续写段所给的提示句进行续写，但续写内容衔接不够紧密<br>3. 会使用背诵的微场景语料的词块、句式等进行续写 |
| 存在障碍 | 1. 不能深入挖掘人物的情感变化，导致写作中出现人物前后表现不一的现象，不能很好地实现人物协同<br>2. 不能准确把握文本的叙述视角和写作风格，导致语言风格和原文缺乏协同性<br>3. 不能很好地挖掘作者的写作意图，主题表达跑偏或与原文缺乏协同性<br>4. 续写内容语言的丰富性欠佳，不能兼顾到动作描写、心理描写、环境描写、语言描写等<br>5. 不能准确使用复杂句式或复杂语料进行续写<br>6. 缺少对读后续写评价标准的深度研读，不能理解读后续写的评价标准，并难以基于评价标准调整自己的写作内容 |

续表

| 项目 | 内容 |
|---|---|
| 发展需求 | 1. 提高语篇的深度研读能力，掌握总结文本的语言风格和人物的形象特点的方法，进而概括和提炼主题意义（what, how, why）<br>2. 在写作的过程中，注重语言协同、人物协同和情节协同，完善写作逻辑，使续写内容在主题和风格上更加贴合原文<br>3. 在特定的主题语境下掌握微场景语料运用的方法，并积累相关语料库<br>4. 能够精准地进行动作、情绪、心理、语言和环境的多维描写，使内容更加生动、具体<br>5. 掌握增强语句间逻辑关系的方法，提高续写内容的连贯性和逻辑性<br>6. 了解评分标准，并根据评分标准修改、润色自己的作品，不断提升写作质量 |
| 解决措施 | 1. 借助可视化的语篇研读方法进行语篇分析，梳理和挖掘表层信息及深层信息（如使用故事山梳理语篇的情节和情感线，结合句子研读、挖掘人物性格等）<br>2. 借助五五拍戏教学法，构建续写框架及丰富的情节<br>3. 借助点线面润色升级法和连句成篇技巧，提升语言表达的丰富性和连贯性<br>4. 对照读后续写评价标准，分析和评价自己的续写内容，并总结经验，实现知识迁移 |

## 三、教学目标

通过本节课，学生能够：

**语言能力**

1. 通过赏析因飞机延误而匆忙赶车的场景，如 run like crazy, jump into the first taxi, without a second thought 等，积累描述赶车场景的词汇，并体会人物的焦急心情。

2. 通过研读相关语句，体会并总结人物性格，学会通过精准用词刻画人物形象（如：① When I was about to give up, Gunter fished out his little phone and rang up a friend. ② Finally, with just two minutes to spare，we rolled into the bus station.）

3. 通过赏析文本的叙述风格，学会使用幽默语言和比喻等修辞手法实现续写内容的语言和情节与原文的协同。

4. 学会运用点线面润色升级法提升语言表达，同时运用连句成篇技巧，增强文章的连贯性。

**文化意识**

1. 通过探讨跨文化场景中给异乡人的善意，思考在国际交往和文化交流中，如何身体力行地充当文明的使者。

2. 通过分析作者诚信还车费的情节，认识诚信的重要性，培养自身的道德修养和诚信意识。

**思维品质**

1. 学会使用可视化工具（如故事山和六何分析法）梳理、分析、概括和整合文本的浅层和深层含义，提升逻辑分析能力。

2. 学会使用五五拍戏教学法构建续写框架，合理组织情节，提升情节设计的逻辑性和丰富性。

**学习能力**

1. 在自评和同伴互评中，提升反思能力和团队协作能力。

2. 熟悉并使用相关的写作策略，将所学知识迁移到后续写作中。

## 四、教学思路

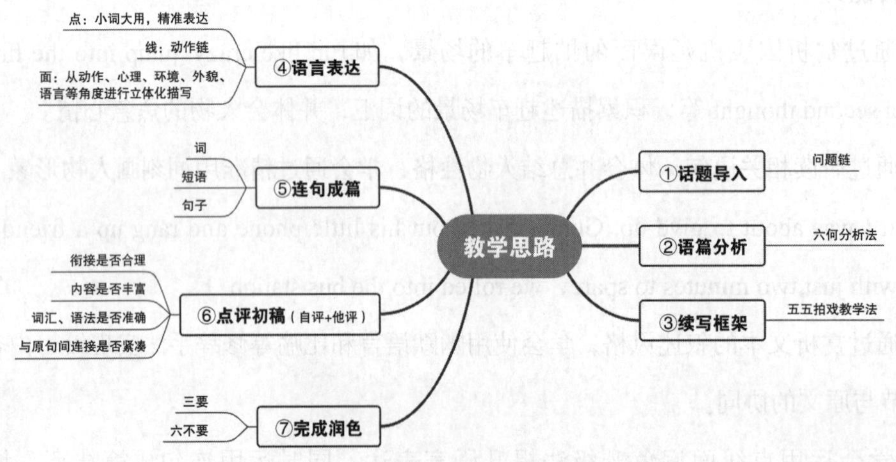

## 五、教学过程

<table>
<tr><th>阶段</th><th>活动形式及步骤</th><th>问题链</th><th>设计意图</th></tr>
<tr><td>话题导入</td><td>1. 创设情境：如果身处异国，语言不通，你又必须赶上最后一班公交车，你要如何去做？<br>2. 呈现图片：面对一个语言不通的出租车司机，你会有什么期待？</td><td>1. What will you do if you must catch the last bus in a totally strange foreign country?<br>2. What expectations will you have if you face a taxi driver who speaks another language?</td><td>通过导入两个与续写文本相关的问题，让学生能够站在主人公的角度思考问题，激活已知</td></tr>
<tr><td rowspan="2">语篇分析</td><td>1. 快速浏览文章，按照六何分析法提取文本浅层信息（when/where/who）<br>语篇分析<br>① “I met Gunter on a cold, wet and unforgettable evening in September. I had planned to fly to Vienna and take a bus to Prague for a conference. Due to a big storm, my flight had been delayed by an hour and a half. I touched down in Vienna just 30 minutes before the departure of the last bus to Prague. The moment I got off the plane, I ran like crazy through the airport building and jumped into the first taxi on the rank without a second thought.<br>六何分析法<br>when: on a cold, wet and unforgettable evening in September<br>where: In Vienna; on my way to catch the last bus to Prague<br>who: I; Gunter, a taxi driver in Vienna<br>what: story mountain<br>how: analyze the narrative perspective and style<br>why: analyze the purpose</td><td>1. When did the story take place?<br>2. Where did the story take place?<br>3. Who were the main characters in the text?</td><td>运用六何分析法，快速提取文本的浅层信息，了解文本大意</td></tr>
<tr><td>2. 借助故事山梳理文本的情节线和情感线（what）<br>情节分析——story mountain【what】<br>Para. 1:<br>• I met Gunter, a taxi driver in Vienna .<br>• I: anxious<br>Para. 2-3:<br>• We spared efforts to reach the bus station hurriedly.<br>• I: nervous; thankful<br>Para. 4-5:<br>• I had difficulty in paying him the fare.<br>• I: desperate<br>Para. 6:<br>• I ran back to tell Gunter the bad news.<br>• sorry; sincere<br>续写：<br>• How would Gunter react and what might be the story ending?<br>• A happy ending?</td><td>1. What was the beginning of the story?<br>2. How did the story develop?<br>3. What was the problem faced by the author?<br>4. What was the resolution of the problem?<br>5. What was the ending of the story?<br>6. How did the author feel in the process?</td><td>运用故事山梳理文本的情节和情感两条线，引导学生关注故事走向和人物的情感变化，为下一步人物分析打下基础</td></tr>
</table>

续表

| 阶段 | 活动形式及步骤 | 问题链 | 设计意图 |
| --- | --- | --- | --- |
| 语篇分析 | 3. 标记出文本中有关主人公的描写和介绍，进行人物分析 (who)<br>**人物分析【who】**<br>I<br>• The moment I got off the plane, I ran like crazy through the airport building and jumped into the first taxi on the rank without a second thought.<br>• I thought my pronunciation was the problem, so I explained again more slowly.<br>• I flashed him an apologetic smile as I pulled out my Portuguese bankcard.<br>• I jumped out of the car, made a mad run for the machine, and popped my card in.<br>**I was responsible and polite, eager to catch the last bus to Prague.**<br>Gunter<br>• When I was about to give up, Gunter fished out his little phone and rang up a friend.<br>• At this moment, Gunter pointed towards the waiting hall of the bus station.<br>**Gunter was enthusiastic, easygoing, kind and willing to solve problems.** | 1. Which sentences can show the characters' personalities?<br>2. Based on the above mentioned sentences, could you conclude the characters' personalities? | 在寻找原文与人物相关语句的过程中，引导学生品鉴相关的动作和心理描写，推断人物的所思所想，为下一步的读后续写做准备 |
| | 4. 分析文本的叙述视角与语言风格（how）<br>**叙述视角与语言风格分析【how】**<br>Narrative perspective<br>• I met Gunter on a cold, wet and unforgettable evening in September.<br>• Due to a big storm, my flight had been delayed by an hour and a half.<br>• That was when I met Gunter. I told him where I was going, but he said he hadn't heard of the bus station.<br>**第一人称视角：I**<br>**回忆性文章：时过境迁后"I"的回忆**<br>Narrative style<br>• The moment I got off the plane, I ran like crazy through the airport building .<br>• When I was about to give up, Gunter fished out his little phone and rang up a friend.<br>• A feeling of helplessness washed over me as I saw the bus queue thinning out.<br>**语言风格：descriptive; vivid; diversified use of verbs and adjectives；humorous** | 1. What is the narrative perspective of the story?<br>2. What is the narrative style of the story? | 从叙述和写作技巧的角度分析、概括文章的写作风格，思考如何在续写任务中保持语言协同 |
| | 5. 提炼、分析文本的情感、态度和价值观 (why)<br>**情感、态度、价值观分析【why】**<br>人与社会<br>A harmonious society builds on people's mutual understanding and kindness.<br>人与自我<br>Once a promise is made, it should be strictly kept. | What values or life perspectives do you think the author wants to convey through the story? | 通过衔接主题语境，引导学生从宏观上确定故事要传达的情感和态度，挖掘其背后的价值观，确定读后续写的主题和立意 |
| 续写框架 | 使用五五拍戏教学法构建一个续写框架（每个段落都续写五个句子，两段续写句子的编号为1~10），并结合情节续写，从承上启下、故事结局和情感、态度、价值观等角度，提供拍戏建议<br>Tip 1：确定演员<br>Tip 2：确定出场顺序<br>Tip 3：戏份不够，细节或环境来凑 | Part 1:What were the main characters in Para. 1 and 2?<br>Part 2:<br>1. What would "I" say after telling Gunter the problem?<br>2. Did "I" catch the last bus according to the first sentence in Para. 2?<br>3. What happened after "I" called Gunter as promised four days later?<br>4. What was the ending of the story? | 提供清晰的续写框架，融合之前的人物分析，引导学生在保证情节协同和语言协同的基础上，构建合理的故事情节 |

续表

| 阶段 | 活动形式及步骤 | 问题链 | 设计意图 |
|---|---|---|---|
| 续写框架 | 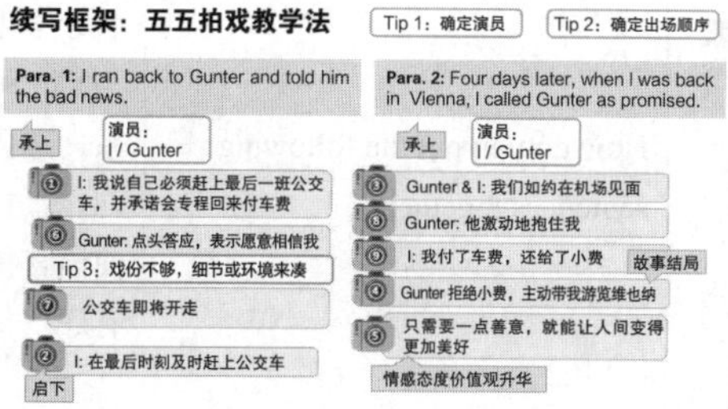 **续写框架：五五拍戏教学法**<br>Tip 1：确定演员 Tip 2：确定出场顺序<br>**Para. 1:** I ran back to Gunter and told him the bad news.<br>承上 演员：I / Gunter<br>I: 我说自己必须赶上最后一班公交车，并承诺会专程回来付车费<br>Gunter: 点头答应，表示愿意相信我<br>Tip 3：戏份不够，细节或环境来凑<br>公交车即将开走<br>I: 在最后时刻及时赶上公交车<br>启下<br>**Para. 2:** Four days later, when I was back in Vienna, I called Gunter as promised.<br>承上 演员：I / Gunter<br>Gunter & I: 我们如约在机场见面<br>Gunter: 他激动地抱住我<br>I: 我付了车费，还给了小费<br>故事结局<br>Gunter 拒绝小费，主动带我游览维也纳<br>只需要一点善意，就能让人间变得更加美好<br>情感态度价值观升华 | 5. What values does the story convey?<br>6. In Para. 1, did Gunter accept my promise?<br>7. Did the bus leave at that moment?<br>8. What would Gunter react when seeing me come back as promised?<br>9. What did I do after meeting Gunter at the airport? | |
| 语言表达 | 1. 结合续写框架，列出十句草稿 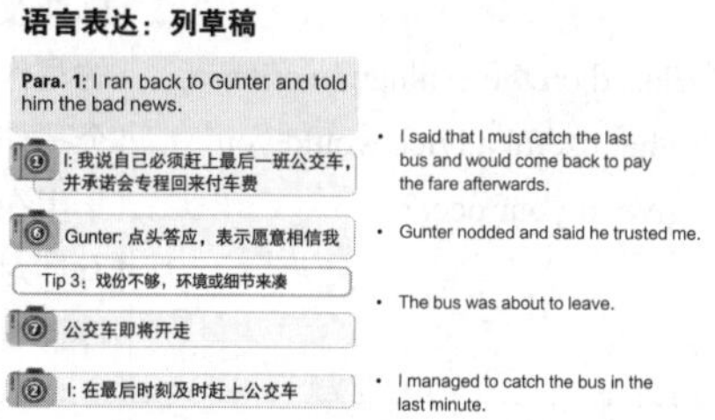<br>**语言表达：列草稿**<br>**Para. 1:** I ran back to Gunter and told him the bad news.<br>I: 我说自己必须赶上最后一班公交车，并承诺会专程回来付车费 • I said that I must catch the last bus and would come back to pay the fare afterwards.<br>Gunter: 点头答应，表示愿意相信我 • Gunter nodded and said he trusted me.<br>Tip 3：戏份不够，环境或细节来凑<br>公交车即将开走 • The bus was about to leave.<br>I: 在最后时刻及时赶上公交车 • I managed to catch the bus in the last minute.<br>2. 借助点线面润色升级法润色草稿，并标记微场景 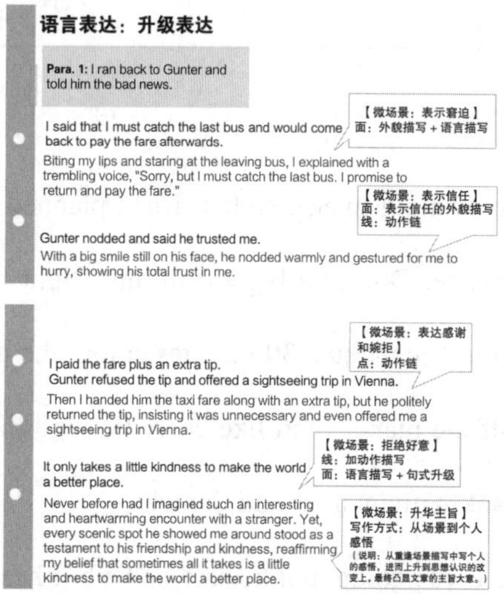<br>**语言表达：升级表达**<br>**Para. 1:** I ran back to Gunter and told him the bad news.<br>I said that I must catch the last bus and would come back to pay the fare afterwards.<br>【微场景：表示窘迫】面：外貌描写 + 语言描写<br>Biting my lips and staring at the leaving bus, I explained with a trembling voice, "Sorry, but I must catch the last bus. I promise to return and pay the fare."<br>【微场景：表示信任】面：表示信任的外貌描写 线：动作链<br>Gunter nodded and said he trusted me.<br>With a big smile still on his face, he nodded warmly and gestured for me to hurry, showing his total trust in me.<br>【微场景：表达感谢和婉拒】点：动作链<br>I paid the fare plus an extra tip.<br>Gunter refused the tip and offered a sightseeing trip in Vienna.<br>Then I handed him the taxi fare along with an extra tip, but he politely returned the tip, insisting it was unnecessary and even offered me a sightseeing trip in Vienna.<br>【微场景：拒绝好意】线：加动作描写 面：语言描写 + 句式升级<br>It only takes a little kindness to make the world a better place.<br>Never before had I imagined such an interesting and heartwarming encounter with a stranger. Yet, every scenic spot he showed me around stood as a testament to his friendship and kindness, reaffirming my belief that sometimes all it takes is a little kindness to make the world a better place.<br>【微场景：升华主旨】写作方式：从场景到个人感悟（说明：从重逢场景描写中写个人的感悟，进而上升到思想认识的改变上，最终凸显文章的主旨大意。） | 1. How would you polish your draft?<br>2. Could you summarize the tips to polish your writing? | 引导学生运用语言的点线面润色升级法，并在仿写的过程中提升写作的模仿和迁移能力，从而提升写作能力 |

续表

| 阶段 | 活动形式及步骤 | 问题链 | 设计意图 |
| --- | --- | --- | --- |
| 连句成篇 | 以“词→短语→句子”循序渐进的方式将润色的十句话连句成篇完成初稿<br>**连句成篇**<br>**请注意连接成分，并进行分类。**<br>连接成分：副词，连词 ①⑦⑨；短语 ②③⑤；句子 ④⑥⑧<br>Para 1: I ran back to Gunter and told him the bad news. Biting my lips and staring at the leaving bus, I explained with a trembling voice: “Sorry, ① but I must catch the last bus. I promise to return and pay the fare.” With a big smile still on his face, he nodded warmly and gestured for me to hurry, showing his total trust in me. ② At the very moment, the bus made a beep-beep sound, with its engine starting to rumble, ready to drive away. ③ Just then, I swiftly jumped onto the bus ④ while he stood outside, waving enthusiastically at me.<br>Para 2: ⑤ Four days later, when I was back in Vienna, I called Gunter as promised. Bathed in the warm sunlight, we met at the bustling airport as planned. ⑥ The moment he saw me, he hugged me like long lost friends and joked, “This is quite a long taxi ride, lasting for four days.” ⑦ Then I handed him the taxi fare along with an extra tip, but he politely returned the tip, insisting it was unnecessary and even offered me a sightseeing trip in Vienna. ⑧ Never before had I imagined such an interesting and heartwarming encounter with a stranger. ⑨ Yet, every scenic spot he showed me around stood as a testament to his friendship and kindness, reaffirming my belief that sometimes all it takes is a little kindness to make the world a better place. | How do you put the following sentences together? | 引导学生研读句与句之间的关系，选择恰当的词、短语和从句，使语言衔接更加有序 |
| 点评初稿 | 结合评价量表进行自评和互评【详见附录一及附录二】 | Based on the evaluation criteria, what useful advice would you give to your peer? | 提供详细的评分标准及三个重要的写作要点和六个写作陷阱，使学生在创作时更有针对性，牢记评价要点 |
| 润色习作 | 结合评价反馈润色自己的习作 | How could you refine your writing based on the feedback? | 结合同伴反馈，润色、完善写作内容 |

## 附录1：真题文本

① I met Gunter on a cold, wet and unforgettable evening in September. I had planned to fly to Vienna and take a bus to Prague for a conference. Due to a big storm, my flight had been delayed by an hour and a half. I touched down in Vienna just 30 minutes before the departure of the last bus to Prague. The moment I got off the plane, I ran like crazy through the airport building and jumped into the first taxi on the rank without a second thought.

② That was when I met Gunter. I told him where I was going, but he said he hadn't heard of the bus station. I thought my pronunciation was the problem, so I explained again more slowly, but he still looked confused. When I was about to give up, Gunter fished out his little phone and rang up a friend. After a heated discussion that lasted for what seemed like a century, Gunter put his phone down and started the car.

③ Finally, with just two minutes to spare, we rolled into the bus station. Thankfully, there was a long queue still waiting to board the bus. Gunter parked the taxi behind the bus, turned around, and looked at me with a big smile on his face. "We made it," he said.

④ Just then I realized that I had zero cash in my wallet. I flashed him an apologetic smile as I pulled out my Portuguese bankcard. He tried it several times, but the card machine just did not play along. A feeling of helplessness washed over me as I saw the bus queue thinning out.

⑤ At this moment, Gunter pointed towards the waiting hall of the bus station. There at the entrance, was a cash machine. I jumped out of the car, made a mad run for the machine, and popped my card in, only to read the message: "Out of order. Sorry."

**注意**

1. 续写词数应为150个左右；
2. 请按如下格式在答题卡的相应位置作答。

I ran back to Gunter and told him the bad news.____________________________

________________________________________________________

Four days later, when I was back in Vienna, I called Gunter as promised.________________

________________________________________________________

## 附录 2：参考范文

**I ran back to Gunter and told him the bad news.** Biting my lips and staring at the leaving bus, I explained with a trembling voice, “Sorry, but I must catch the last bus. I promise to return and pay the fare.” With a big smile still on his face, he nodded warmly and gestured for me to hurry, showing his total trust in me. At the very moment, the bus made a beep-beep sound, with its engine starting to rumble, ready to drive away. Just then, I swiftly jumped onto the bus while he stood outside, waving enthusiastically at me.

**Four days later, when I was back in Vienna, I called Gunter as promised.** Bathed in the warm sunlight, we met at the bustling airport as planned. The moment he saw me, he hugged me like long lost friends and joked, “This is quite a long taxi ride, lasting for four days.” Then I handed him the taxi fare along with an extra tip, but he politely returned the tip, insisting it was unnecessary and even offered me a sightseeing trip in Vienna. Never before had I imagined such an interesting and heartwarming encounter with a stranger. Yet, every scenic spot he showed me around stood as a testament to his friendship and kindness, reaffirming my belief that sometimes all it takes is a little kindness to make the world a better place.

# 第十节

# 以 2024 年九省联考卷为例的读后续写教学设计案例

## 一、文本分析

**What** 本文的主题语境是“人与社会”，涉及“良好的人际关系与社会交往”的内容。文章主要描述了志愿者 Hilda 在海洋公园清洁海豚池的经历。在一次清洁过程中，一只名叫 Maya 的海豚将一张糖果包装纸带出水面，这导致 Hilda 因工作疏忽而遭到训练员 Katherine 的指责。为了查明真相，Hilda 决定提前到公园潜水搜查，并观察 Maya 的行为。最终， Hilda 发现 Maya 一直在秘密收集池中的各种物品。

续写第一段的段首句：“这就是 Maya 的小秘密，” Hilda 微笑着说道。

续写第二段的段首句：Katherine 现在意识到发生了什么。

根据续写两段的段首句内容，可以预测后面的故事情节：Hilda 和 Katherine 消除了误会，Katherine 则充分了利用 Maya 的聪明才智改进训练方法。训练结果非常出色，整个海洋公园充满了欢声笑语。

**Why** 本文通过描述 Hilda 在被误解与指责后主动探寻真相的经历，引导读者在面对困难时应该保持冷静，理性思考，并积极寻找解决问题的方法。Hilda 用实际行动证明了自己的清白，展现了她的探索精神和责任感，同时她观察 Maya 的行为也凸显了人与动物之间互动的趣味。

**How** 本文以第三人称视角，采用生动的动作描写（如 swimming playfully, stopped suddenly, stuck her nose down 等）、丰富的心理活动描写（如 wondered，confused 等）、深刻的情感描写（如 upset but not discouraged）和具体的语言描写（如“I know where she got it," declared Hilda. "Maya! Where did you get that?" demanded Katherine.），讲述了一个引人入胜的故事。

## 二、学情分析

**基本信息：高二学生；班级人数：45 人；平均分：90 分左右；读后续写平均分：15 分左右。**

| 项目 | 内容 |
|---|---|
| 已有基础 | 1. 基本了解记叙文的语篇结构和语言特征<br>2. 能梳理出文本大意并获取简单的细节信息<br>3. 能用简单的句子进行语言表达 |
| 存在障碍 | 1. 不熟悉海洋馆主题的相关词汇<br>2. 不能厘清故事脉络，导致续写内容走向偏离原文<br>3. 不能准确分析、挖掘故事的人物特征，导致续写内容与原文不协同 |
| 发展需求 | 1. 完善与海洋馆相关的背景知识和主题词汇语义网<br>2. 学习并练习如何根据原文情节和风格进行故事续写，以确保续写内容与原文风格一致且情节发展自然<br>3. 提高动作、环境、外貌和心理描写等技能，丰富续写内容 |
| 解决措施 | 1. 创设真实的语言环境，了解海洋馆海豚与工作人员之间的互动交流<br>2. 借助可视化的六何分析法开展语篇分析，把握故事核心要素<br>3. 借助五五拍戏教学法助力搭建续写框架，使得故事情节与原文协同<br>4. 通过点线面润色升级法丰富动作、环境、外貌、心理等方面的描写 |

## 三、教学目标

通过本节课，学生能够：

**语言能力**

1. 通过分析 Hilda、Katherine 和海豚 Maya 互动的细节，学会使用生动的动词短语和描述性语言提升描写的生动性和具体性。

2. 通过赏析 Hilda 的心理活动，掌握如何通过细腻的心理描写展现人物的内心世界。

**文化意识**

1. 通过分析 Hilda 积极面对误解并解决问题，理解在生活中遇到困难时保持冷静并积极寻找解决方案的重要性，培养解决问题的意识和能力。

2. 通过分析 Hilda 与团队的互动，认识到团队合作和信任在问题解决中的关键作用，树立尊重和理解他人的合作意识。

**思维品质**

1. 借助六何分析法开展语篇分析，提炼故事核心要素和叙事逻辑，提升逻辑推理和信息整合能力。

2. 借助五五拍戏教学法构建续写框架，培养逻辑推理能力。

3. 借助点线面润色升级法探索丰富人物行为和语言表达的多样性方法，培养批判性和创新性思维。

**学习能力**

通过自主探索和小组合作完成续写任务，提升信息处理能力、团队合作意识和独立学习能力。

## 四、教学思路

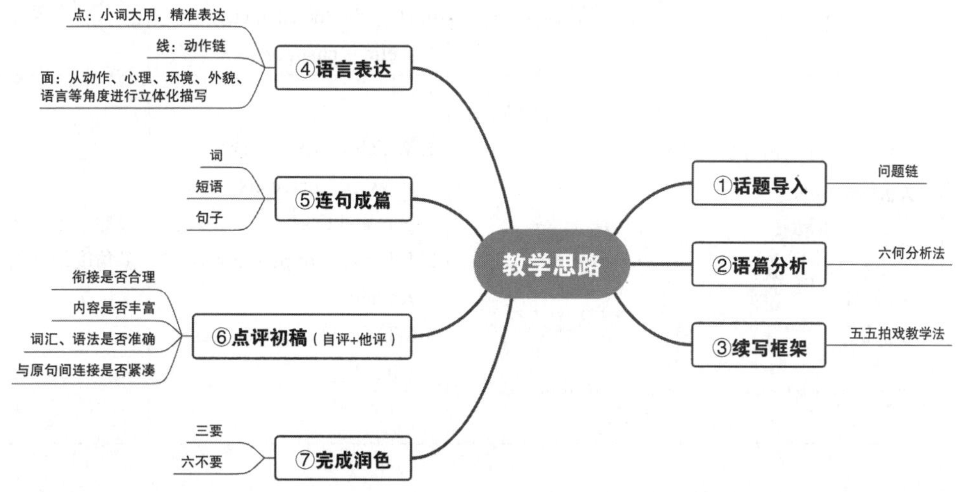

## 五、教学过程

| 阶段 | 活动形式与步骤 | 问题链 | 设计意图 |
| --- | --- | --- | --- |
| 话题导入 | 观看一段海洋馆训练师训练海豚的视频，回答相关问题 | 1. What do you see in the video?<br>2. How do the dolphins interact with the trainer in the video? | 通过视频展示，给学生提供海洋馆和海豚生活的背景知识，为后续的阅读和续写活动奠定基础 |
| 语篇分析 | 1. 小组合作使用六何分析法梳理文本的浅层信息（when/where/who）<br>**语篇分析**<br>① Last summer, Hilda worked as a volunteer with dolphin trainers at a sea life park. Her job was to make sure the tanks were free of any items so that the trainers could train the dolphins to fetch specific items. However, one day after cleaning, one of the dolphins, Maya, presented Hilda with a candy wrapper from the tank. When Katherine, the trainer, saw this, she blamed Hilda for her carelessness. Upset but not discouraged by this event, Hilda decided to do some spying on Maya.<br>**六何分析法**<br>when: last summer; what: story mountain<br>where: at a sea life park; how: analyze the narrative perspective and style<br>who: Hilda, Maya, Katherine; why: analyze the purpose | 1. When did the story take place?<br>2. Where did the story take place?<br>3. Who were the main characters in the story? | 帮助学生快速掌握故事的背景和主要人物特点，为深入分析文本并完成续写任务奠定基础 |
| | 2. 使用故事山梳理故事的情节线和情感线（what）<br>**情节分析——story mountain【what】** 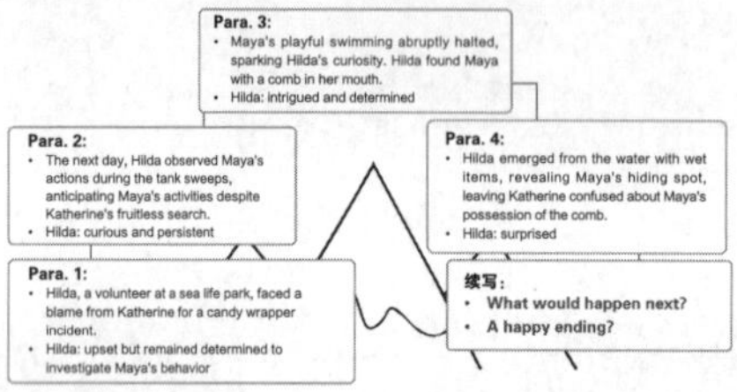<br>Para. 1:<br>• Hilda, a volunteer at a sea life park, faced a blame from Katherine for a candy wrapper incident.<br>• Hilda: upset but remained determined to investigate Maya's behavior<br>Para. 2:<br>• The next day, Hilda observed Maya's actions during the tank sweeps, anticipating Maya's activities despite Katherine's fruitless search.<br>• Hilda: curious and persistent<br>Para. 3:<br>• Maya's playful swimming abruptly halted, sparking Hilda's curiosity. Hilda found Maya with a comb in her mouth.<br>• Hilda: intrigued and determined<br>Para. 4:<br>• Hilda emerged from the water with wet items, revealing Maya's hiding spot, leaving Katherine confused about Maya's possession of the comb.<br>• Hilda: surprised<br>续写：<br>• What would happen next?<br>• A happy ending? | 1. How did the story start?<br>2. How did the story develop?<br>3. What was the main conflict in the story?<br>4. How was the conflict resolved?<br>5. How did the story end?<br>6. How did the characters' feelings change? | 加深学生对故事情节发展和人物情感变化的理解，帮助学生在续写时合理地延续情节线和情感线 |
| | 3. 回读文本，标记出文本中有关主人公的描写和介绍，进行人物分析 (who)<br>**人物分析【who】**<br>Hilda<br>• Hilda was upset but not discouraged by Katherine's blame for the candy wrapper incident.<br>• Hilda decided to do some spying on Maya.<br>Hilda was determined, resilient, and persistent.<br>Katherine<br>• When Katherine, the trainer, saw this, she blamed Hilda for her carelessness.<br>• As Katherine turned around, her mouth dropped open.<br>Katherine was strict and expressive. | 1. Which sentences can show the characters' personalities?<br>2. What kind of person was Katherine?<br>3. What kind of person was Hilda? | 引导学生有逻辑、多角度地分析人物性格 |

续表

| 阶段 | 活动形式与步骤 | 问题链 | 设计意图 |
| --- | --- | --- | --- |
| 语篇分析 | 4. 分析文本的叙述视角和语言风格 (how)<br>叙述视角与语言风格分析【how】<br>Narrative perspective<br>• Last summer, Hilda worked as a volunteer with dolphin trainers at a sea life park.<br>• Maya, presented Hilda with...<br>• When Katherine, the trainer, saw this, she...<br>第三人称视角：Hilda，Maya，Katherine<br>Narrative style<br>• She stuck her nose down behind the box and then swam away.<br>• ...with a handful of items still wet from their watery, resting place.<br>• ...at the edge of the tank with a comb in her mouth waiting for her treat.<br>语言风格：descriptive，detailed | 1. From whose viewpoint is the story told?<br>2. How does the author's writing style contribute to the narrative? | 引导学生识别并分析文本的叙述视角和语言风格，确保续写语言协同 |
| | 5. 小组探究文本的情感、态度和价值观 (why)<br>情感、态度、价值观分析【why】<br>人与社会：<br>The narrative highlights the importance of perseverance, curiosity, and a positive attitude in overcoming obstacles and finding effective solutions. | 1. What is the theme of the story?<br>2. What values does the author want to convey?<br>3. What can we learn from the story? | 加深学生对文本主题、作者情感和背后价值观的理解，确保在续写活动中能够有效延续和发展这些核心要素 |
| 续写框架 | 借助五五拍戏教学法搭建续写框架。使用五五拍戏教学法构建一个续写框架（每个段落都续写五个句子，两段续写句子的编号为 1~10），并结合情节续写，从承上启下、故事结局和情感、态度、价值观等角度，提供拍戏建议<br>Tip 1：确定演员<br>Tip 2：确定出场顺序<br>续写框架：五五拍戏教学法<br>Tip 1：确定演员　Tip 2：确定出场顺序<br>Para. 1: "This is Maya's secret," Hilda said with a big smile.<br>承上　演员：Hilda & Katherine<br>① Hilda & Katherine：Hilda 向 Katherine 展示 Maya 收集的各种物件<br>⑥ Katherine：Katherine 询问<br>⑦ Hilda：Hilda 向 Katherine 解释<br>⑧ Katherine：Katherine 感到惊讶<br>② Katherine：对 Hilda 赞叹 Maya 的聪明<br>启下<br>Para. 2: Now Katherine realized what had been going on.<br>承上　演员：Hilda & Katherine & Maya<br>③ Katherine：向 Hilda 道歉<br>⑨ Hilda：表示谅解<br>⑩ Katherine：Katherine 转向 Maya，拍了拍她<br>④ Katherine & Maya：Katherine 决定在训练中加入 Maya 独特的天赋　故事结局<br>⑤ 在接下来的日子里，Maya 热情地向每个人展示她的秘密收藏，整个海洋公园每天都充满了欢乐的笑声<br>情感、态度、价值观升华 | Part 1:<br>What were the main characters in Para. 1 and 2?<br>Part 2:<br>1. What is Maya's secret?<br>2. What might Katherine do upon learning the secret?<br>3. What might Katherine do after learning what had been going on?<br>4. What was the ending of the story?<br>5. What values does the story convey?<br>6. What might Katherine react when she saw the things Maya collected?<br>7. How would Hilda explain everything?<br>8. How did Katherine feel upon learning the secret?<br>9. How did Hilda respond to Katherine's sincere apology?<br>10. What did they do then? | 引导学生借助五五拍戏教学法搭建合理的续写框架 |

续表

| 阶段 | 活动形式与步骤 | 问题链 | 设计意图 |
| --- | --- | --- | --- |
| 语言表达 | 1. 依托搭建好的框架，撰写草稿<br>**语言表达：列草稿**<br>**Para. 2:** Now Katherine realized what had been going on.<br>⑧ Katherine：向 Hilda 道歉<br>⑨ Hilda：表示谅解<br>⑩ Katherine：Katherine 转向 Maya，拍了拍她<br>④ Katherine & Maya：Katherine 决定在训练中加入 Maya 独特的天赋<br>⑤ 在接下来的日子里，Maya 热情地向每个人展示她的秘密收藏，整个海洋公园每天都充满了欢乐的笑声<br>• "I'm sorry I misunderstood you, Hilda," she apologized.<br>• "It's okay. I'm just glad we figured it out together." Hilda replied.<br>• Katherine turned to Maya, and gave her an affectionate pat. "You're a smart girl, Maya," she said.<br>• Katherine decided to incorporate Maya's unique talent into their upcoming training sessions.<br>• Maya enthusiastically presented her secret collections to everyone, the entire sea life park echoing with laughter every day.<br>2. 使用点线面润色升级法对以上草稿进行表达升级，并梳理和升级思路<br>**语言表达：升级表达**<br>**Para. 2:** Now Katherine realized what had been going on.<br>"I'm sorry I doubted you, Hilda," she apologized. 【微场景：道歉】面：+心理描写（独立主格）<br>"I'm sorry I didn't believe you, Hilda," Katherine apologized, her eyes showing her regret and gratitude.<br>"It's okay. I'm just glad we figured it out together." Hilda replied. 【微场景：谅解】线：动作链<br>Hilda smiled warmly and said, "It's okay. I'm just glad we found out the truth together."<br>Katherine turned to Maya, and gave her an affectionate pat. "You're a smart girl, Maya," she said. 【微场景：表示夸赞】面：+动作描写（+状语）<br>Katherine turned to Maya, and gave her an affectionate pat. "You're a smart girl, Maya," she said, as Maya responded cheerfully. | How will you polish the sentences? | 引导学生从点、线、面三个不同的方面将草稿进行升级润色，使句子更加生动、饱满 |
| 连句成篇 | 借助"词→短语→句子"方法将润色后的句子连句成篇<br>**连句成篇**<br>**请注意连接成分，并进行分类。**<br>连接成分：词 ①③；短语 ④；句子 ②⑤<br>**Paragraph 1:** "This is Maya's secret," Hilda said with a big smile. She ① then displayed a variety of objects Maya had collected, including a colorful key chain and a small mirror. "How did she do that?" Katherine asked. "Each of these must have caught her eyes during our training sessions," Hilda explained, her voice filled with relief and amazement. ② As Katherine leaned closer and examined the items, she was impressed by Maya's cleverness. "It seems we've underestimated her, Hilda," her earlier anger turning into fascination.<br>**Paragraph 2:** Now Katherine realized what had been going on. "I'm sorry I misunderstood you, Hilda," she apologized ③ sincerely. "It's okay. I'm just glad we figured it out together." Hilda replied with a smile. Katherine turned to Maya, and gave her an affectionate pat. "You're a smart girl, Maya," she said, as Maya responded cheerfully. ④ Inspired by Maya's cleverness, Katherine decided to incorporate Maya's unique talent into their upcoming training sessions, enhancing both their performances and their mutual respect. ⑤ In the days that followed, Maya enthusiastically presented her secret collections to everyone, the entire sea life park echoing with laughter every day. | How do you put the above sentences together? | 运用"词→短语→句子"的方法，使语言衔接更加有序 |
| 点评初稿 | 利用评价量表开展自评和互评，指出习作优点和不足，并填写改进建议【详见附录一及附录二】 | What advice will you give to your peer? | 利用细化的评价标准帮助学生厘清自己作文的优点和存在的问题，以便修改、润色 |
| 润色习作 | 结合评价反馈润色、修改课堂习作 | How could you refine your writing based on the feedback? | 落实、巩固学生课堂所学的语言框架和微技能 |

## 附录 1：真题文本

① Last summer, Hilda worked as a volunteer with dolphin trainers at a sea life park. Her job was to make sure the tanks were free of any items so that the trainers could train the dolphins to fetch specific items. However, one day after cleaning, one of the dolphins, Maya, presented Hilda with a candy wrapper from the tank. When Katherine, the trainer, saw this, she blamed Hilda for her carelessness. Upset but not discouraged by this event, Hilda decided to do some spying on Maya.

② The next morning, Hilda arrived at the park early. She put on her scuba gear (水下呼吸器) and jumped into the tank for her usual, underwater sweep. Finding nothing in the tank, she climbed out of the water just in time to see Katherine jumping in on the other side. After what happened yesterday, Hilda knew what she was doing. She watched as Katherine performed her underwater search, but Hilda wasn't surprised when she surfaced empty-handed.

③ During the tank sweeps, Maya had been swimming playfully, but now the dolphin stopped suddenly and swam to the back part of the tank where the filter ( 过滤 ) box was located. She stuck her nose down behind the box and then swam away. What was Maya doing back there? Hilda wondered. She jumped back into the water and swam over to take a look behind the box, and her question was answered. Hilda then swam across the tank following Maya's path and emerged from the water to find Katherine removing her scuba gear. As Katherine turned around, her mouth dropped open. There was Maya at the edge of the tank with a comb ( 梳子 ) in her mouth waiting for her treat.

④ "Maya! Where did you get that?" demanded Katherine, taking the comb and throwing her a fish. "I know where she got it," declared Hilda climbing out of the tank with a handful of items still wet from their watery, resting place. "What's all this?" Katherine asked, obviously confused.

**注意**

1. 续写词数应为 150 个左右；
2. 请按如下格式在答题卡的相应位置作答。

"This is Maya's secret," Hilda said with a big smile. ________________________

______________________________________________________________________

Now Katherine realized what had been going on. ____________________________________

______________________________________________________________________

附录 2：参考范文

**"This is Maya's secret," Hilda said with a big smile.** She then displayed a variety of objects Maya had collected, including a colorful key chain and a small mirror. "How did she do that?" Katherine asked. "Each of these must have caught her eyes during our training sessions," Hilda explained, her voice filled with relief and amazement. As Katherine leaned closer and examined the items, she was impressed by Maya's cleverness. "It seems we've underestimated her, Hilda," her earlier anger turning into fascination.

**Now Katherine realized what had been going on.** "I'm sorry I misunderstood you, Hilda," she apologized sincerely. "It's okay. I'm just glad we figured it out together." Hilda replied with a smile. Katherine turned to Maya, and gave her an affectionate pat. "You're a smart girl, Maya," she said, as Maya responded cheerfully. Inspired by Maya's cleverness, Katherine decided to incorporate Maya's unique talent into their upcoming training sessions, enhancing both their performances and their mutual respect. In the days that followed, Maya enthusiastically presented her secret collections to everyone, the entire sea life park echoing with laughter every day.

# 录一 读后续写评分标准

| 评分档次 | 第一项 | 第二项 | 第三项 | 第四项 |
|---|---|---|---|---|
| 第五档<br>(21-25 分) | 与所给短文融合度高，与所提供的各段落开头语衔接合理 | 内容丰富 | 语法结构和词汇丰富、准确，可能有些许错误，但完全不影响意义的表达 | 有效地使用了语句间的连接成分，全文结构紧凑，意义连贯 |
| 第四档<br>(16-20 分) | 与所给短文融合度较高，与所提供的各段落开头语衔接较合理 | 内容比较丰富 | 语法结构和词汇较为丰富、准确，可能有些许错误，但不影响意义的表达 | 比较有效地使用了语句间的连接成分，全文结构紧凑，意义比较连贯 |
| 第三档<br>(11-15 分) | 与所给短文关系较为密切，与所提供的各段落开头语有一定程度的衔接 | 写出了若干相关内容 | 语法结构和词汇能够满足任务要求，虽有一些错误，但不影响意义的表达 | 运用简单的语句间的连接成分，全文结构基本紧凑，意义基本连贯 |
| 第二档<br>(6-10 分) | 与所给短文有一定关系，与所提供的各段落开头语有一定程度的衔接 | 写出了少数相关内容 | 语法结构单调，应用词汇有限，有些语法结构与词汇错误影响意义的表达 | 较少使用语句间的连接成分，全文结构欠紧凑，意义欠连贯 |
| 第一档<br>(1-5 分) | 与所提供的短文和开头语的衔接较差 | 产出内容过少 | 语法结构单调，词汇很少，有较多语法结构和词汇方面的错误，严重影响意义的表达 | 缺乏语句间的连接成分，全文结构不紧凑，意义不连贯 |

# 附录二

## 读后续写学生自[illegible]



| | | |
|---|---|---|
| 三要 | 1. 内容、语言要一致 | |
| | 2. 情节要完整 | |
| | 3. 结局要正能量满满 | |
| 六不要 | 1. 尽量不要新增人物 | |
| | 2. 不要使用过多对话 | |
| | 3. 不要设置负能量结局 | |
| | 4. 不要文末设悬念 | |
| | 5. 不要偏离主题 | |
| | 6. 不要违背逻辑常理 | |